The Complete Sailing Guide

In the same series:

The Complete Windsurfing Guide
The Complete Cycle Sport Guide
The Complete Microlight Guide
* The Complete Hang Gliding Guide

* *in preparation*

EP Publishing Limited

Roland Denk

The Complete
SAILING
Guide

About the Author

Since 1965 Roland Denk, a talented sports instructor, has devoted himself to his special subject — sailing. His experiences derive not only from his enthusiasm as a cruising yachtsman and racing sailor but also from being the head sailing instructor of a large sailing school (at the Sports Centre of Munich's Technical University).
He was (and still is) very active in the German Sailing Association in many fields: as a trainer (to 1976), as a contributor to work done on instructor training techniques, as a member of the examination committee, and as chief technical editor of the sailing teaching programme. To date Denk has written nine books on sailing.

Originally published in German under the title *Neue Segelschule Vom Anfänger zum Führerschein — A/A1*
Copyright © 1981 BLV Verlagsgesellschaft mbH, Munich

First English edition 1983

English translation copyright © 1983 EP Publishing Limited

ISBN 0 7158 0829 X (casebound)
       0 7158 0830 3 (paperback)

Published by EP Publishing Limited, Bradford Road, East Ardsley, Wakefield, West Yorkshire, WF3 2JN, England

British Library Cataloguing in Publication Data

Denk, Roland
    The complete sailing guide.
    1. Sailing
    I. Title   II. Neue Segelschule. *English*
    797.1'24   GV811

ISBN 0-7158-0829-X

Cover photograph: All-Sport
All other photographs by the author

Design: Anton Walter
Cover design: Krystyna Hewitt

Illustrations: Barbara von Damnitz

Translation: Wendy Gill

Typeset in 9pt Univers by The Word Factory, Rossendale, Lancashire.

Printed and bound in Italy by
Legatoria Editoriale Giovanni Olivotto, Vicenza.

Contents

Foreword

With the help of specially chosen photographs and clear diagrams we have produced this book for everyone who is interested in sailing, a book written with the following clear objectives:

1. It contains all the basic information and practical exercises to set beginners on the right path to becoming good sailors.
2. The book does not simply repeat all the old ideas but is concerned with new and improved modern sailing techniques, as used today by all good sailors — naturally from the point of view of a methodical teaching programme.
3. As well as a basic grounding in theory, the book concentrates on the practical aspects of sailing clearly and in depth.
4. This is the first sailing guide to include a 'teach yourself' programme. This tried and tested programme will help the student sailor to master the various manoeuvres in as short a time as possible.

The book is not only an ideal textbook for sailing students, but also a guide for more experienced sailors. It will contribute a great deal to your 'sailing education' in a most important way: it will help increase your enjoyment on the water (it is true that the better your technique the greater your enjoyment), and also help to keep the ever popular busy sailing areas safe (remember that the more skilful you are, the safer you can be).

Finally, a note on the text: technical expressions are printed in italics so they can be easily recognised. Expressions or words which need special emphasis are in bold type.

I wish you every success in your sailing.

Roland Denk

1 The Boat

Types of Boat

Boats can be divided into motor boats and sailing boats. The latter can be sub-divided into two groups, **single-hulled boats** and **multihulls**. Catamarans and trimarans are multihulls. A **catamaran** has two narrow hulls joined by a bridge construction lying above the water. A **trimaran** has a larger centre hull supported on either side by two shorter side hulls similar to outriggers. Multi-hulls have no ballast, their width giving them stability, and they are noted for their high speeds. However, in strong winds they can capsize.

The more common single-hulled boats can be divided into two categories:

- Centre-board boats and
- Keelboats.

Centre-board boats are also called **dinghies**. In general they are smaller than keelboats and have a centre-board which can be raised up. They have the advantage that they can be taken into shallow waters and can be stored ashore. Their stability is reasonably good, but they can capsize if they heel too far since the centre of gravity lies above the water surface. Capsizing, in general, presents no problems since the boat is unsinkable, and most ding-hies can easily be righted.

Larger dinghies with cabins which are suitable for longer journeys are called **dinghy cruisers**. The smaller and flatter light dinghies used especially for *planing* are called **planing dinghies**.

Keelboats, also called *yachts*, have a permanent keel which is ballasted with lead, iron or concrete. The centre of gravity, therefore, lies below the water surface which means yachts cannot

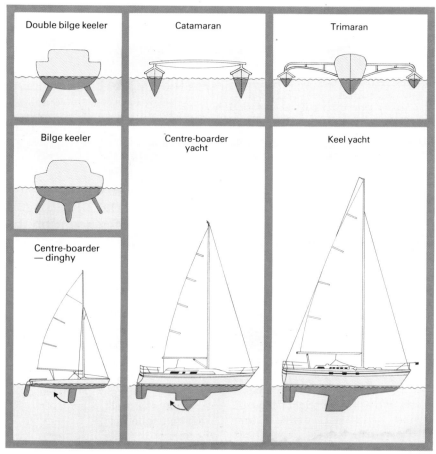

Double bilge keeler

Catamaran

Trimaran

Bilge keeler

Centre-boarder yacht

Keel yacht

Centre-boarder — dinghy

capsize. The more they roll over to the side (*heel*) the more the righting force is brought into play. It is, of course, very comforting to know you cannot capsize, but remember that a yacht full of water can sink!

A yacht with a cabin, and therefore suitable for longer journeys, is called a **cabin cruiser**. If there is no cabin structure and the boat has only a deck, we talk of a **flush-decked yacht**. If there is no cabin at all we talk of an **open keelboat**. A popular mixture is the **centre-boarder yacht**, which has a shorter ballasted keel containing a centre-plate. The advantage of this type of boat, which is mainly used for inland and inshore sailing, is the smaller draught when the centre-plate is raised. An even newer mixture is the **ballasted centre-boarder**, a larger dinghy with a heavy centre-plate which reduces the risk of capsizing.

Today, we also find yachts with bulb keels which can be raised like dagger-boards. These are known as **drop keelers**. Less common types of keel yachts are those with **twin bilge keels** or a **centre keel with bilge keels either side**. These boats have a smaller draught and will stay upright if they run aground — an advantage which makes them popular in tidal creeks and estuaries.

From time to time we come across *bilge centre-board dinghies*. These dinghies provide more room in the cockpit because there are two centre-board cases, one on either side of the boat, instead of just one in the middle. It is true that this gives more room, but it also reduces the good sailing qualities of the boat.

Summary

Bilge keeler: Short centre keel with two additional bilge keels. If there is no centre keel it is called a *twin bilge keeler*.
Catamaran: Twin-hulled yacht.
Centre-boarder yacht: Keelboat with shorter ballasted keel and also a centre-plate.
Cruiser: Yacht with cabin suitable for longer journeys.
Dinghy: Boat with a centre-board which can be raised.
Dinghy cruiser: Centre-boarder with cabin.
Drop keeler: Keelboat with a ballasted keel that can be raised.
Keelboat: Also called a *yacht*, with a permanent ballasted keel.
Trimaran: Three-hulled boat.
Yacht: General expression used to describe any sailing boat. Keelboats are often called 'yachts' to distinguish them from dinghies.

Boat Construction

Materials

The following materials are most commonly used in boat construction: natural wood, bonded thin wood laminates, fibreglass, steel, aluminium, plywood and ferro-concrete.

The oldest and most widely used material through the ages has been **natural wood**. It has a long life, but requires care in maintenance. Since wood contracts or expands when it dries out or gets wet, leaks can occur. Waterproof hulls moulded from **thin wood laminates** do not distort and produce lighter, leak-proof boats. This material is very popular for racing boats. **Steel** is stronger but also heavier than wood and is sometimes used for cruising yachts. Steel boats need quite a lot of attention to keep corrosion and rust in check. Light and rustproof **aluminium** is extremely popular for fast, offshore racing yachts. However, it is very expensive and tends to suffer from galvanic corrosion. **Ferro-concrete** is becoming increasingly popular in the construction of some larger yachts, especially by amateur builders.

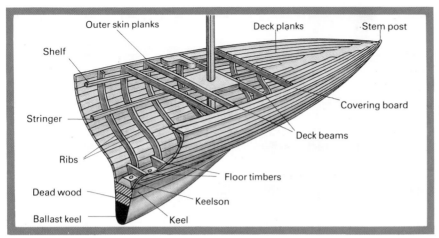

1. **Clinker construction** with overlapping planks.
2. **Carvel construction** with the planks lying edge to edge giving a smooth surface.

The places where the planks are joined together fore and aft are called *seams*, and the vertical joins in the individual planks are called *joints*.

Sometime lengthwise battens are placed along the inside of the seams of the carvel-built construction. The **diagonal carvel construction** gives an especially solid outer skin. This double plank construction requires far fewer internal frames and stringers.

The hot moulded wood construction method consists of bonding several layers of thin wood laminates round a mould and curing by heat.

Synthetics

Glass-reinforced plastics are incorporated in the construction of the modern fibreglass boats, normally using the **hand layering method**. A smooth female mould is covered with a release agent and then a thin layer of thin polyester resin to which pigments and colour have been added is applied. This *gel coat* eventually forms the outer skin. After it has hardened, several layers of fibreglass tissue, matting and woven rovings are applied, each being 'wetted out' with resin until the required hull thickness is obtained. Finally, the whole is left to cure. The deck, moulded separately, is bonded and bolted to the hull.

Today the most popular construction method is that using Glass Reinforced Polyester (fibreglass), which consists of a mixture of polyester resin and fibreglass matting bonded together. The material is easy to shape, watertight, durable in sea water, noncorrosive and easy to maintain. However, it does suffer from surface pitting and *osmosis*, a chemical ailment nicknamed 'boat pox'.

If two different materials are used, e.g. wood planks on steel ribs, the boat is said to be of **composite construction**.

Natural Wood

A framework of lengthwise and cross timbers is made from individual planks.

The **keel** forms the foundation and backbone with **bow and stern posts**. On yachts the **ballast keel fin** is bolted under the keel. The **ribs** are fixed to the keel at the **floor timbers**. Often the keel has a strengthening timber sitting on it called the **keelson**. The boat is reinforced fore and aft by **stringers** which join the ribs together. The uppermost stringer, which also forms a surface for the **deck beams**, is called the **shelf**. The planks forming the deck lie along the beams, the outermost planks forming the **covering board**.

The hull may be divided by partitions — **bulkheads** — and may have a flat timber at the stern called the **transom**.

There are two basic types of plank construction:

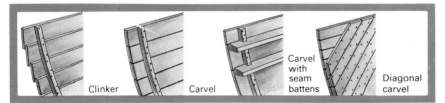

Clinker   Carvel   Carvel with seam battens   Diagonal carvel

Sometimes balsa or foam cores are laid between the two fibreglass layers to form a sandwich. This type of boat is very rigid, and is so well insulated that condensation is greatly reduced.

Summary

Carvel construction: Method of construction where the planks are placed edge to edge forming a smooth surface.

Carvel construction with seam battens: Type of carvel-built boat with ribbon-like timbers along the inside of the seams.

Clinker construction: Construction method using overlapping planks.

Crosswise connecting timbers: Ribs, floor timbers, deck beams, bulkheads, transom.

Cure: Harden off G.R.P. in a temperature of 50°–60°.

Fore and aft connecting timbers: Keel, keelson, stern post, stringer, stem post, shelf.

Gel coat: Special mixture of resin and colour to form the outer skin of a fibreglass boat.

G.R.P.: Glass-reinforced polyester.

Joint: The vertical join in an individual plank.

Keel: The lowest timber running fore and aft, forming the 'backbone'.

Keelson: Strengthening timber on the keel.

Polyester: Most commonly used resin in 'plastic' constructions.

Seam: Joint between two planks running fore and aft.

Stem and stern posts: The timbers forming the extremities of the boat fore and aft.

The Hull

Hull Shapes

The different types of boat mentioned at the beginning of the book, dinghy, yacht, catamaran, trimaran, etc., can have different hull shapes when seen in cross-section. The most common of these are: Sharpie (flat-bottomed hard chine is the simplest), hard chine, double hard chine, round bilge, round section, trapezoid and V-shaped (see diagram). The Optimist is a typical example of a flat-hulled boat, the Pirate and Star are typical hard chine boats. Dinghies such as the Corsair have a round bilge, and typical round-bilge boats would be the Dragon and the Nordic folkboat.

Some offshore racing yachts have the modern trapezoid frame.

Hard chines give the boat good stability; it is described as being stiff. A narrow hull means a less stable boat

with a tendency to heel; it is said to be tender. However, this type of boat is easier to handle in waves, because it slices through them.

Seen from the side, the surface of the hull which is below the water and stops the boat making leeway is called the *plane of lateral resistance*. The greater part of the plane of lateral resistance is provided by the centre-board on a dinghy and by the keel on a yacht. There are very many different types of hull profiles found on yachts ranging from long and streamlined to very cut-away. A long, streamlined lateral plane gives the boat good lateral stability and is recommended for larger cruisers. However, the speed will suffer as a result of the larger surface of lateral resistance. Modern fast racing yachts have very cut-away lateral planes.

If the curve of the deck fore and aft (the **sheer**) is concave, i.e. the lowest point lies in the centre of the deck with an upward slope towards bow and stern, we talk of a *positive sheer*. If the deck slopes down at bow and stern we have a *negative sheer* (see p. 12).

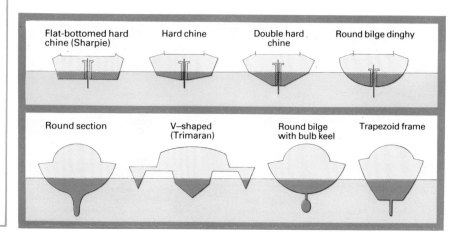

Flat-bottomed hard chine (Sharpie) Hard chine Double hard chine Round bilge dinghy

Round section V–shaped (Trimaran) Round bilge with bulb keel Trapezoid frame

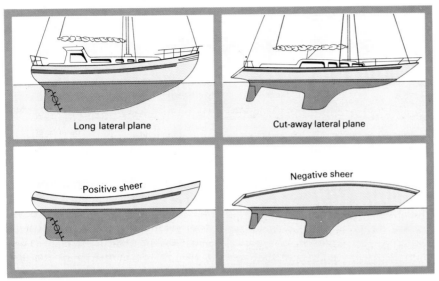

Long lateral plane

Cut-away lateral plane

Positive sheer

Negative sheer

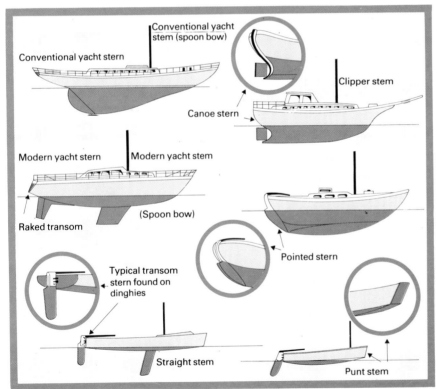

Conventional yacht stern

Conventional yacht stem (spoon bow)

Clipper stem

Canoe stern

Modern yacht stern

Modern yacht stem

Raked transom

(Spoon bow)

Pointed stern

Typical transom stern found on dinghies

Straight stem

Punt stem

Bow and Stern Shapes

The part of the boat at the very front of the bow is called the **stem** and this can have many different shapes. The **straight stem**, which is most com monly found on dinghies, sinks deep into the waves since there is very little buoyancy. The **yacht stem**, also called a **spoon bow**, is common on yachts and overhangs the water to a greater or lesser extent. A large overhang will hit the waves hard and cause a lot of spray. The smaller overhang found on modern yachts gives an additional lift and elongates the water-line when the boat heels over, which is important as far as the critical speed is concerned. Less common are the **clipper stem** and the flat **punt stem**.

There are also many different shapes of stern. These include the overhanging **yacht stern**, the **transom stern** typical of dinghies, the pointed **canoe stern** with the rudder underneath, and the rudder-carrying **pointed stern**. The **transom** may be vertical or raked. Modern yachts have sterns that are angular rather than overhanging. They are often squared off with the transom slanting outwards towards the water-line.

Centre-board and Rudder

Instead of a ballasted keel, a dinghy has a retractable centre-board which is placed in the **centre-board case**. The centre-board case sits on a narrow slit in the keel and comes well above the water-line. The centre-board itself may **pivot** when in place (by means of the *centre-board tackle* and sometimes by an *up and down haul line*), or on very

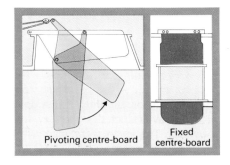

Pivoting centre-board

Fixed centre-board

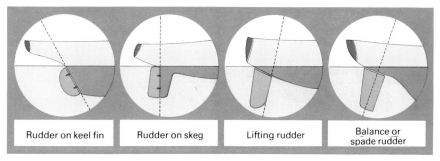

Rudder on keel fin | Rudder on skeg | Lifting rudder | Balance or spade rudder

simple dinghies it may be **fixed** and held firm by a narrow centre-board case when in place. The pivoting type of centre-board has a distinct advantage: if the dinghy should run aground, the centre-board will be pushed up and escape damage.

On a dinghy the entire rudder apparatus is, as a rule, attached to the stern, and the rudder blade can usually be raised by means of a rudder halyard. Since most modern rudders are very light and tend to float upwards, a downhaul is necessary to pull the rudder down and hold it in place.

Fixed rudders may either be situated on the keel fin itself, i.e. on a rudder tail fin (*skeg*), or it may hang free, in which case it is called a **lifting rudder**, or, if part of the rudder surface lies in front of the turning point, a **balance** or **spade rudder**.

The individual components of the rudder apparatus on a dinghy are: *rudder blade, rudder stock, rudder head, tiller, tiller extension,* and for a lifting rudder a *halyard* or *blade up and down haul line.*

Instead of a rudder halyard an up and down haul line is often used. Often a downhaul only is used for light wooden or plastic rudders.

More Terminology

The part of the bow and stern which lies over the water is called the **overhang**. The boat itself floats with the water surface on its **water-line** (WL). This may be different from the water-line calculated by the boat manufacturer, which is called the **designed water-line** (DWL). The length of that part of the boat which does not overhang is the **length of the water-line** (LWL) and this is important for the critical speed. The water-line is the dividing line between the **under-water hull** and the **freeboard**. The **overall length** is the total length including the overhangs, and the **overall beam** is the total width as opposed to the **water-line width** (WLW). The **deck curve** is the curvature of the deck across the boat, the **sheer**, as already mentioned, being the deck curve fore and aft. The space occupied by the crew is called the **cockpit**. And finally the space between the floor and the keel is the **bilge**.

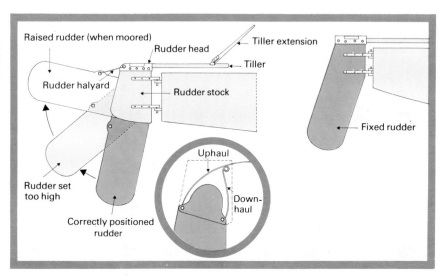

Raised rudder (when moored)
Rudder head
Tiller extension
Tiller
Rudder halyard
Rudder stock
Rudder set too high
Correctly positioned rudder
Uphaul
Down-haul
Fixed rudder

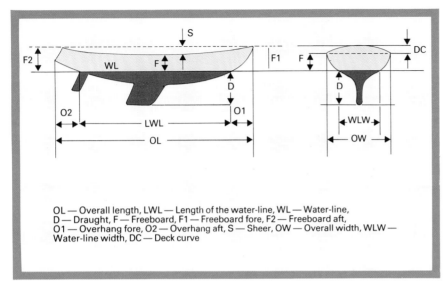

OL — Overall length, LWL — Length of the water-line, WL — Water-line, D — Draught, F — Freeboard, F1 — Freeboard fore, F2 — Freeboard aft, O1 — Overhang fore, O2 — Overhang aft, S — Sheer, OW — Overall width, WLW — Water-line width, DC — Deck curve

Rigging

Rigging is a collective term for all the equipment on board used to sail a boat:
- Mast and spars.
- Mast supports — standing rigging.
- The equipment used to set or trim the sails — running rigging.

Many experts include the sail itself in the rig.

Mast, Spars, Standing Rigging

The modern aluminium mast must be supported so it can withstand the strength of the wind. Mast supports are made from good, rustproof stainless steel wire. A distinction is made between the **shrouds**, which run from the side of the boat to the sides of the mast (port shroud and starboard shroud) and the **stays**, which run from the bow (*forestay*) and stern (*backstay*) to the front and back of the mast. The larger the boat and the mast, the greater the tension on both the shrouds and the stays. As a rule small boats only have one port and one starboard shroud and one forestay. Larger yachts sometimes have a **babystay** as well as *lower, centre, upper* and *cap shrouds*. A backstay may be replaced by *preventer backstays*, which have to be repositioned when going about and gybing.

The small one-man Finn-dinghy or Laser boats have no support at all for their extremely flexible masts. The mast supports constitute the **standing**

Summary

Beam: We distinguish between *overall beam* and *water-line width*.

Bilge: Space between floor and keel.

Bow types: Yacht stem or spoon bow, straight stem, clipper stem, square stem.

Centre-board: The flat board placed on the centre-board case on a dinghy to lessen leeway. There are fixed and pivoting centre-boards.

Cockpit: Space occupied by crew.

Deck curve: Curve of the deck across the boat.

Freeboard: Height of the sheerline of the boat above the water-line.

Hull shapes: Sharpie, hard chine, double hard chine, round, V-shaped, trapezoid.

Lateral plane: The sideways view of the underwater hull.

Length: We distinguish between total length — *overall length*, and the length excluding overhangs — *length of the water-line*.

Overhang: The part of bow and stern overhanging the water.

Rudder types: Fixed rudder, lifting rudder, balance or spade rudder, and the lifting rudder commonly used on dinghies.

Sheer: Curve of the deck fore and aft.

Stern types: Yacht stern, square stern, canoe stern, pointed stern.

Underwater hull: The part of the boat under the water.

Water-line: The water surface line on the side of the boat. The water-line calculated by the manufacturer of the boat is the *designed water-line*.

rigging. *Rigging* the boat means putting the mast in place and attaching the standing rigging, *de-rigging* being the opposite. This has nothing to do with *hoisting* or *lowering* the sails which is usually what the layman means.

The mast can be positioned so that it is completely vertical or has a slight tilt aft (called the **rake**). The shrouds are attached to the boat by means of **shroud plates**, and they are tensioned by means of **screw terminals**. On larger yachts the tension of the backstay can be regulated by means of a special adjusting wheel, or hydraulics.

Spars are all the other 'round poles' found on board, which are usually made from aluminium: the main boom (sometimes also mizzen-boom), jib boom, spinnaker boom and the spreaders on the mast itself (spreader — cross pole to spread the shrouds apart).

Running Rigging

The running rigging includes all the lines used to hoist, take in, reef, set and trim the sails, to position the rudder and centre-board and also to hoist a flag. They are called the halyards and sheets, the tensioners, the kicking strap, the flag lines, the topping lift and the boom preventer. The **topping lift** is a line running over a roller at the *masthead* to the *boom end* to take the weight of the boom when taking in or reefing the sails. The **boom preventer** is a line running from the boom end forwards to prevent the boom swinging over when sailing before the wind in heavy seas.

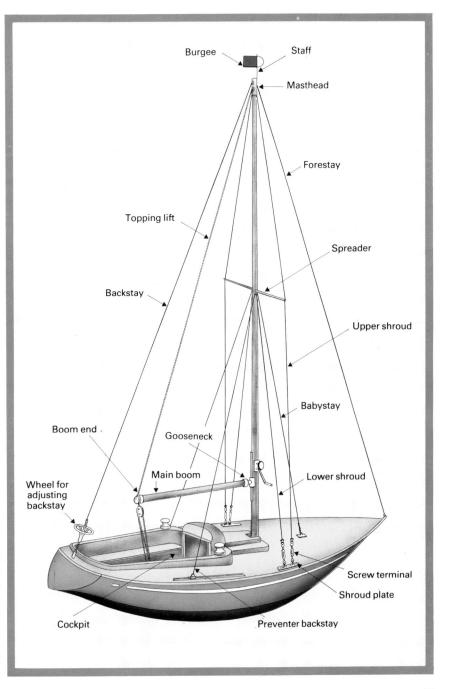

Burgee
Staff
Masthead
Forestay
Topping lift
Spreader
Backstay
Upper shroud
Babystay
Boom end
Gooseneck
Lower shroud
Wheel for adjusting backstay
Main boom
Screw terminal
Shroud plate
Cockpit
Preventer backstay

A **tack tensioner** may be used to stretch the mainsail luff by pulling down the boom at the gooseneck. The *gooseneck* is the fitting which attaches the boom to the mast and which may run up and down the mast on a track. Some modern racing boats also have a *cunningham hole* which helps to regulate the mainsail luff tension. The cunningham eyelet is found above the tack eyelet (see diagram p.19) through which a tensioning line runs.

The **halyards** used to hoist the sails (main halyard and jib halyard) are normally made of rope with a wire lead-in section. On large yachts they may be made entirely of wire. The mainsail is adjusted by means of the **mainsheet**, and the jib is adjusted by means of the **jibsheet**.

Pulley systems are normally used to make the handling of the running rigging easier. This combination of blocks and ropes is called a **handy-billy** (the non-sailor would say 'block and tackle').

There are *running parts* which move between the blocks, *fixed parts* which stay in one place, and *hauling points* which are the parts the sailor pulls on. Some blocks simply change direction with no mechanical advantage.

Mechanical advantage is usually expressed as a ratio, e.g. 2:1 means that the moving end of the system pulls twice as hard as the force applied by the operator, 3:1, three times as hard, etc.

Types of Yachts

Yachts are classified by the number and grouping of the sails and masts. Three types of rigging have only one mast while three different forms of rigging have two masts.

The simplest rigging of all is known as the **cat** or U.N.A. rig. This has one mainsail only with no jib. Most one-man dinghies are cats, e.g. the Finn-dinghy or Laser. If a jib is added we have a **sloop-rig** and if the boat has two foresails we are talking about a **cutter**.

Larger yachts often have two masts. These yachts are classified according to the size and position of the aftermost mast. If this is smaller than the main mast it is called a **mizzen-mast** and if it stands inside the designed water-line, i.e. in front of the rudder, the yacht is known as a **ketch**. If the mast is smaller and stands outside the designed water-line, i.e. behind the rudder, the yacht is a **yawl**. If the aftermost mast is larger than the fore mast (or the same length) it is classed as the *main mast*, and the front mast becomes the *jib* or *foremast* (**schooner**).

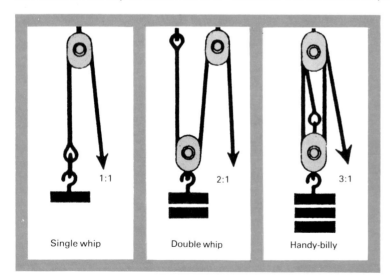

Single whip   Double whip   Handy-billy

Summary

Cat: Simplest rigging — one mainsail only.

Cutter: Rigging with two foresails.

De-rig: Free the standing and running rigging and remove the mast. Opposite: *rig.*

Halyard: Rope to raise the sail (also centre-board and rudder).

Handy-billy: Combination of ropes and blocks ('block and tackle').

Ketch: Two-master, aftermost mast smaller and inside designed water-line — in front of rudder.

Rigging: Collective term for mast and main boom, also the associated standing and running rigging.

Running parts: The ropes running over blocks or fairleads.

Schooner: Two-master, larger aftermost sail.

Shroud: Wire used for sideways support of the mast.

Shroud plate: Fitting on the side of the boat on which to fasten the shroud lanyard.

Sloop: One-master with mainsail and foresail.

Spars: 'Poles' such as main, spinnaker and jib booms, and spreader.

Standing rigging: Metal wires used to support mast.

Stays: Metal wires — part of the standing rigging, to support the mast fore and aft.

Yawl: Two-master, smaller aftermost mast outside the designed water-line, and behind the rudder.

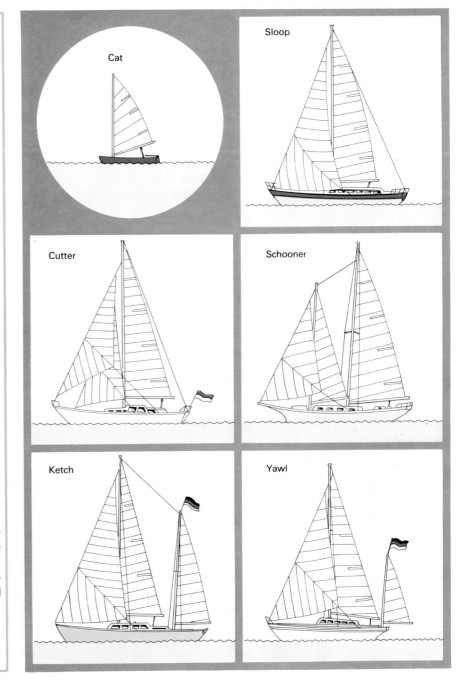

Cat

Sloop

Cutter

Schooner

Ketch

Yawl

Sails

Manufacture

Modern sails are made from man-made fibres (called by different terms according to where the material is manufactured, e.g. Dacron in the U.S.A., Terylene in the U.K., Tergal in France), and no longer from pure cotton.

Advantages include better propulsion and less chance of tearing; these sails also keep their shape longer, are water repellant, and can be stored wet in the sail bag without losing shape or becoming mildewed (a good sailor, however, will always hang a wet sail up to dry!). The sailmaker achieves the correct profile (i.e. the required curvature) by using a specialised technique to cut the individual pieces of cloth. The panels may run across the sail (mainsail) or they can run diagonally (foresail). Spinnakers are made from especially light cloth (e.g. nylon) and many different types of cutting techniques are used.

Types of Sail

There are two main types of sail: the square sail and the triangular sail. The upper bolt rope of a square sail is fastened to the spars, the so-called yards, which lie across the mast. This was the type of sail used by the old windjammers, but today it is only normally found on large naval training ships such as the *Winston Churchill*, or on small dinghies such as a yacht tender or the Optimist dinghy.

Modern sporty sailing boats have three-cornered sails where the luff is vertical to the mast. There are several different types:
1. **Bermudian sail:** This is the most popular sail today. Its advantage lies in its three-cornered high cut: the longest leading edge is to the wind, making this type excellent for sailing close-hauled.
2. **Gaff-sail:** This sail, which is not as popular as the Bermudian, has a gaff spar near the top of the mast that can be raised and lowered by means of two halyards. Because of the shorter mast a gaff-sailed boat is especially suitable for areas with many bridges.

3. **Lug-sail:** This sail, which is still occasionally found on small boats, is similar to the gaff-sail in having a top spar, but, unlike the gaff-sail, it extends a little beyond the mast.
4. **Lateen-sail:** Every holidaymaker on the Mediterranean will recognise this sail, widely used by the local fishermen, by its long yard.
5. **Sprit-sail:** This is the typical sail used on Optimist dinghies. It has four corners with a diagonal spar (called, in this case, a *sprit*).

Mainsail and Foresail

The **mainsail** is attached to the back of the mast (on boats with more than one mast it is attached to the main mast) and is usually triangular. Its rear edge (**leech**) is usually slightly curved. Batten pockets are sewn into the leech to take battens. Without these battens the leech would *lift* (i.e. curl over) when sailing.

The front and lower edges (**luff** and **foot**) are strengthened with rope which enables the foot or luff to fit into the groove of the mast or boom. There are several other systems by which the

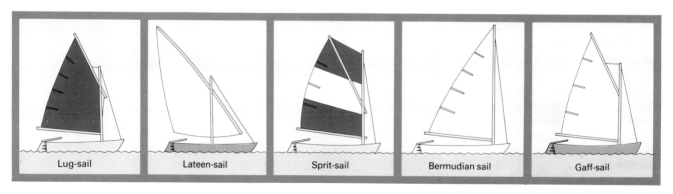

| Lug-sail | Lateen-sail | Sprit-sail | Bermudian sail | Gaff-sail |

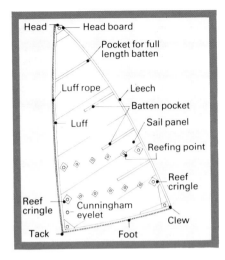

foot and luff can be slid along the boom or mast groove.

The three corners are called the **head** (top), **tack** (near the mast) and **clew** (aft). Many racing sails will have a cunningham about 20 – 30 cm above the tack which can be pulled towards the tack by means of a rope, tensioning the luff and therefore flattening out the sail. If the sail is to be reefed by tying (which is usual on cruisers and offshore racing yachts) there will be two rows of **reefing points** through which the **reefing lines** will run. The first and last of these on the luff and leech are greatly strengthened and are called **reef cringles**.

The foresail in front of the mainsail is called the **jib**. It is also usually triangular and is strengthened on the luff with a sewn-in rustproof cable. Some jibs have fittings (*hanks*) on the luff which can be hooked on to the forestay. The jib is usually smaller than the main-

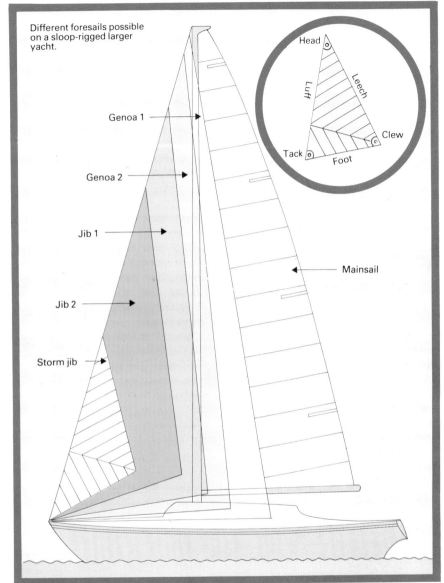

Different foresails possible on a sloop-rigged larger yacht.

sail, especially on dinghies. However, modern yachts often have a foresail which reaches right to the mast head and may have a greater sail area than the mainsail itself. A large foresail with a very long foot is called a *Genoa*, whereas an extremely small foresail is known as a *storm jib*.

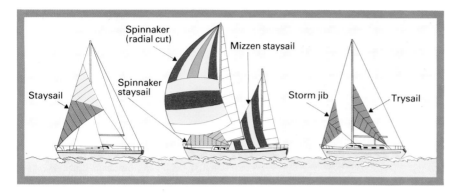

Staysail · Spinnaker (radial cut) · Spinnaker staysail · Mizzen staysail · Storm jib · Trysail

If well-equipped, the larger cruising yacht and, naturally, the offshore racing yacht will carry several types of foresail on board to be prepared for all weather conditions: One large and one small jib (jibs 1 and 2), one storm jib, one large Genoa (Genoa 1) overlapping the mast and one smaller Genoa (Genoa 2). A cutter has a foresail and a staysail.

More Terminology

Sails which are not attached to the mast like the mainsail, but to a stay, are called **staysails**. These include all *foresails, spinnakers* and, on ketches, the *mizzen staysail* between the two masts.

The standard sails on a sloop are the *mainsail* and *jib*. However, other sails might be used in addition to or instead of these two sails. The most common of these additional sails is the **spinnaker** and all the spinnaker-associated sales used in offshire racing (e.g. *Big Boy* and *Blooper*, or the *spinnaker staysail*). In extremely stormy conditions the **trysail** may be used. This is a storm sail, raised in place of the mainsail, with a loose foot, i.e. not attached to the boom.

Summary

Additional sails: Sails additional to or instead of the standard sails, e.g. spinnaker or mizzen staysail.

Bermudian sail: Modern three-cornered mainsail reaching to the masthead.

Corners: The three corners of a sail are called the head (top), tack (near the mast) and clew.

Foot: The edge of the sail along the bottom.

Foresail: A sail attached to a stay in front of the mast: storm jib Genoa, jib and staysail.

Genoa: A very large foresail which overlaps the mast.

Hanks: Small hooks on the luff of many foresails to hook onto the forestay.

Jib: The normal foresail.

Leech: The edge of the sail furthest from the mast.

Loose-footed sail: Sail with foot attached at tack and clew only, including the following types: Bermudian sail, Gaff-sail, Lug-sail, Lateen-sail and Sprit-sail.

Luff: The edge of the sail nearest the mast.

Mainsail: The sail attached to the mast (or main mast).

Reef cringles: Strengthened eyelets on leech and luff on a mainsail to be used when reefing.

Reef points: Small eyelets in a mainsail to be used for points reefing, the reefing lines being fed through the holes.

Sail manufacture: Today made from synthetics only. Curvature obtained by means of specialised cutting techniques (panels run across on a mainsail and usually diagonal on a foresail).

Square sail: As the name suggests, four-cornered. Its upper bolt-rope is fastened to a spar.

Standard sails: The normal sails of any type of boat without any additional sails, e.g. mainsail and jib on a sloop.

Staysail: Sail attached to a stay: all foresails, spinnaker-associated sails, the mizzen staysail.

Trysail: A storm sail to replace the mainsail.

Anchoring

One of the most important items of equipment on a sailing boat (especially a yacht) is the anchor. There are many different types of anchor, all with their own advantages depending on the type of boat and the nature of the seabed.

Basically, there are two types of anchor, the **heavy anchors** which rely mainly on their weight as the holding factor (the traditional stock or Admiralty anchor), and the **lightweight anchors** whose shape rather than weight determines their holding ability and whose ease of handling is also important. The **stock anchor** with the cross-piece (stock) at the top of the shank is still used today as it holds well on stony and weedy ground. Its disadvantage, however, is that it has to be extremely heavy since it digs itself in with one fluke only. The other fluke projects upwards and there is a danger of it snagging lines or chains. The light weight types of anchor, on the other hand, have no projecting parts; the flukes have a large surface area and tend to dig themselves deeper and deeper into the ground, especially if it is soft and sandy.

The most common anchors found on yachts (cruising yachts) are the **Danforth**, **Baas-ball** and **ploughshare** types such as the 'C.Q.R.'.

Dinghies usually have smaller **folding umbrella**-type anchors which stow easily.

Cruising yachts making long journeys should always have two anchors on board — ideally one stock anchor and one Danforth or Baas-ball. An anchor must always be heavy enough for the boat, and this should be borne in mind when buying a new one.

A long **chain** or **hawser** is attached to the anchor. A hawser (line) should only be used on smaller boats (dinghies). For larger yachts especially when sailing any distance from the shore, it is essential to have a chain or at least a hawser with part chain. The chain lead-in should be at least 5m long.

The weight of the chain pulls the anchor to the ground and ensures a satisfactory holding angle. It also prevents the anchor from landing too hard and perhaps breaking loose. The chain will prevent the line from being chafed if the anchorage is rocky.

Summary
Two basic types of anchor: heavy anchors (stock or Admiralty) and lightweight anchors (Danforth, ploughshare, Baas-ball). For dinghies: folding anchors such as the folding umbrella. Important equipment: chain or hawser for dinghies. Compromise between hawser and chain: lead-in chain must be at least 5m long.

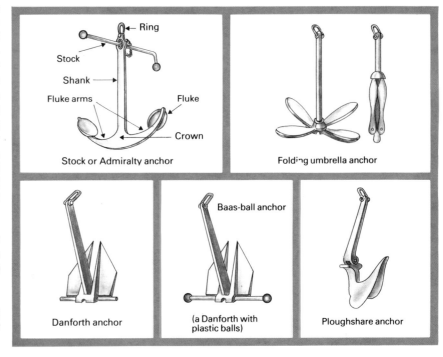

Stock or Admiralty anchor

Ring
Stock
Shank
Fluke arms
Fluke
Crown

Folding umbrella anchor

Danforth anchor

Baas-ball anchor
(a Danforth with plastic balls)

Ploughshare anchor

Equipment

Fittings and Basic Equipment

Fittings include all equipment connected with the boat or rigging which are necessary for the handling of the boat. They may be made from wood, plastic or metal.

Blocks

A block consists of a casing and a pulley through which a rope runs. The most widely used blocks are either single or double pulley blocks, and these are usually made from wood, metal or nylon. A block with a ratchet locking device to one side (often adjustable) is called a *ratchet block*. It will stop a line running back.

Shackles

Small metal loops with closing bolts made from galvanised iron, brass or stainless steel of many different types and sizes. They are used on board to attach different parts together.

Winch

Depending on their size winches may or may not have a handle. They are used for tightening sheets. The barrel round which the rope is wound once or twice can only be turned one way; a safety pawl prevents it from slipping back.

Tensioning Lever

This is a device sometimes used to achieve satisfactory tension, e.g. on halyards or backstays.

Cleats and Bitts

Made from various materials and used for belaying the shrouds or halyards. A strong cleat may also be used as a bitt. Since they have to withstand a great deal of strain, they must be very securely attached (strengthened under the deck).

Jam Cleats and Clam Cleats

These are used to hold a line in position either by the action of two cams that grip the line or by a pinching action when the line is jammed into a serrated slot.

Bottle Rigging Screw

This is a tension screw used to fasten the standing parts to the *chain plate* and to enable it to be adjusted. *Shroud adjusters* do the same job but are much lighter and are used mainly on light dinghies.

Reefing Claw

Horseshoe-shaped loop to slip on to the boom to which the upper block for the mainsheet is shackled. Only found today on older types of boats.

Jibsheet Fairlead

The jibsheet is fed through the fairleads on either side of the boat. The fairleads are usually adjustable and allow the foresail to be trimmed. The most usual kind consist of a track and slider with fairleads, blocks or rollers.

Eyelet

Circular to heart-shaped, made from steel, brass, bronze or nylon, and used to strengthen a hole, e.g. in sails or ropes. An eye spliced in a rope will withstand chafing if an eyelet is used.

Traveller

A fixture running over the cockpit in which a mainsheet block can be moved to windward or leeward in the traveller groove. The angle of the main sheet can thus be adjusted, enabling the mainsail to be trimmed.

Self-bailer

Small valve built into the floor of the cockpit with a non-return valve which can be opened to empty the boat while sailing.

Cooking and Toilet Facilities

Cruising yachts usually have a small *galley* (small kitchen with cooker and sink) and also a toilet.

The cooker should normally run on methylated spirit, paraffin or gas. Petrol should never be used as it is too dangerous on board. Propane gas is also very dangerous being heavier than air. If there were a leak or a faulty connection the gas would sink and collect in the bilge. This could be unintentionally ignited leading to an explosion and horrific results.

Therefore:
- Only use cookers with safety ignition.
- After cooking close the main valve on the bottle immediately.
- Place the gas bottle in an enclosed area with its own ventilation.

You must also be very careful when using methylated spirit or paraffin. For example, never refill when the oven has been lit or is still hot.

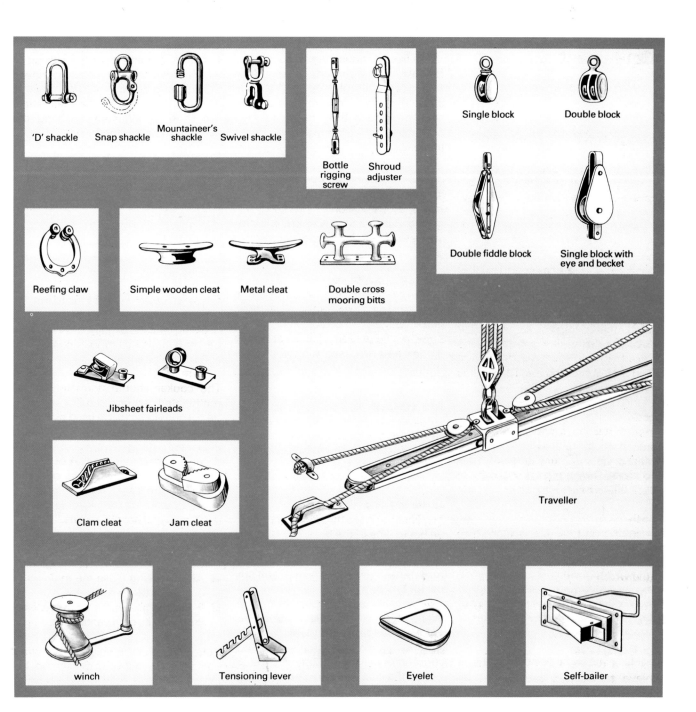

'D' shackle

Snap shackle

Mountaineer's shackle

Swivel shackle

Bottle rigging screw

Shroud adjuster

Single block

Double block

Double fiddle block

Single block with eye and becket

Reefing claw

Simple wooden cleat

Metal cleat

Double cross mooring bitts

Jibsheet fairleads

Clam cleat

Jam cleat

Traveller

winch

Tensioning lever

Eyelet

Self-bailer

23

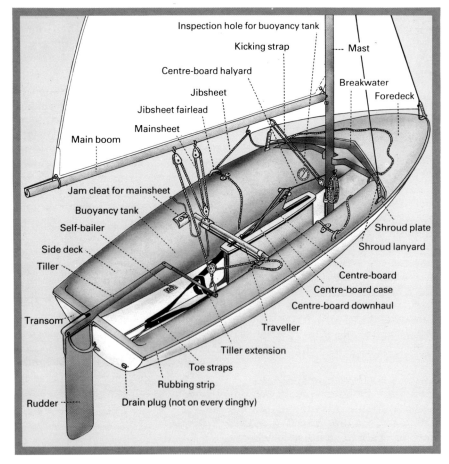

Inspection hole for buoyancy tank
Kicking strap
Mast
Centre-board halyard
Breakwater
Jibsheet
Foredeck
Jibsheet fairlead
Mainsheet
Main boom
Jam cleat for mainsheet
Buoyancy tank
Shroud plate
Self-bailer
Shroud lanyard
Side deck
Tiller
Centre-board
Centre-board case
Centre-board downhaul
Transom
Traveller
Tiller extension
Toe straps
Rubbing strip
Rudder
Drain plug (not on every dinghy)

from rubber or rope, or even inflatable P.V.C. tubing.

Boats with a motor or cooking facilities must carry a *fire extinguisher*, usually of the powder type.

It would be impossible to give a full description of safety equipment necessary for a sea-going yacht here. If necessary you may obtain a copy of *Safety Guidelines (International and National Guidelines for the Equipment and Safety of Ocean-Going Yachts)* published by the Royal Yachting Association, which contains a comprehensive list.

There are also safety rules to observe with a **Yacht W.C.** with an outlet to the sea, i.e. the outlets and inlets must have sea cocks which are only opened when in use (the same applies to sinks). For obvious reasons a Yacht W.C. should never be used on inland lakes or in harbour!

An alternative to the pump-type W.C. is the chemical W.C. or one which has its own storage tank.

Safety Equipment

Important safety equipment — and not just for cruising yachts — excluding the obligatory life-jacket (about which there will be more later), includes *one or two paddles, fenders, boathook*, and to keep the bilge empty *bilge pumps* and a *bucket* for bailing out. Fenders, which protect the side walls from other boats, quay walls or lock walls, may be made

A summary of the safety equipment required for a dinghy is given below:

Boat Classes

Sailing boats can be grouped in different classes. Competitions are only practicable if all the boats taking part are of the same type or if specific rules are laid down regarding the types of boats which can be entered. In general, every sailing boat belongs to one of the following groups: first of all they will be classified according to method of construction:

One-design Classes
These boats are built to carefully controlled plans and regulations. Measurements, weight, form, building materials and other details are precisely laid down. Examples: 470, 420.

Restricted or Development Classes
Here there are often significant differences in the measurements, the weight and the area of sail. A special table is used to equalise these differences. Examples: the Olympic yacht 5.5 or the small Moth.

Handicap Classes
In this class sailing boats (offshore racing yachts) of very different designs can sail against each other, each having a different handicap calculated from handicap tables. The most famous tables are the international I.O.R. Handicap Tables for Racing Yachts.

Level Rating Classes
These are I.O.R. classes sailing with no handicap. The name 'Level Rating' is a

reference to the history of the class. There are mini-, quarter-, half-, three-quarter-, and one- and two-tonners.

Catamaran Classes
There is a separate classification for double-hulled boats. Racing catamarans are internationally divided into Division A (one-man boats), B and C (two-man boats), and D (three-man boats). The maximum measurements for the area of sail, i.e. length and breadth, are laid down. A well known Division B catamaran is the Shearwater and the Tornado is now an Olympic Catamaran Class.

Another method of classification is according to the distribution of the type of boat, or official recognition by a sailing union.

International Classes
These classes are spread over many countries and are controlled by the International Yacht Racing Union (I.Y.R.U.) Well known members are F.D., 470, 505 and Fireball.

National Classes
These are found in one country only. In England they are controlled by the Royal Yachting Association. Well known English classes include Merlin-Rocket, Albacore and Osprey.

Handicap Class Racing
This is a preliminary stage before becoming a recognised national or foreign class. A mass-produced boat may be admitted to this class if it fulfils several conditions. For example: a class committee must be set up, a set of class rules and regulations must be

Minimum safety equipment for small one-man dinghies (e.g. Laser)

Life-jacket or buoyancy aid
Tow line
Paddle

Minimum safety equipment for planing dinghies (e.g. 470, F.D., Corsair)

Life-jacket for each person on board
Tow line
Paddle
Bucket

Minimum safety equipment for larger dinghies

Life-jacket for each person on board
Tow line
Paddle
Anchor with line
Bailer or bucket

Recommended additional equipment for 'normal' planing dinghies

Anchor with line
Bailer or bucket

Recommended additional equipment for larger dinghies

Second paddle, boat hook, bailing pump, signal horn or pipe, red flare or torch, first aid equipment, several fenders.

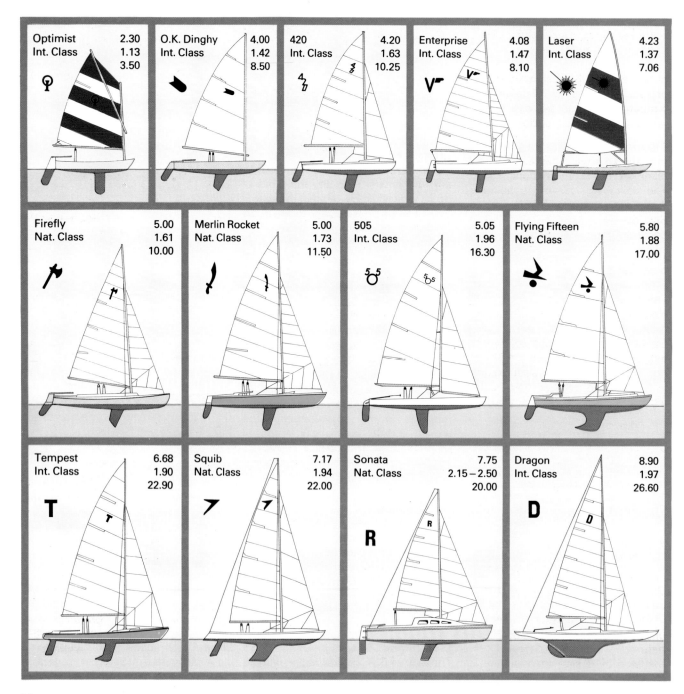

Optimist	Int. Class	2.30 / 1.13 / 3.50
O.K. Dinghy	Int. Class	4.00 / 1.42 / 8.50
420	Int. Class	4.20 / 1.63 / 10.25
Enterprise	Int. Class	4.08 / 1.47 / 8.10
Laser	Int. Class	4.23 / 1.37 / 7.06
Firefly	Nat. Class	5.00 / 1.61 / 10.00
Merlin Rocket	Nat. Class	5.00 / 1.73 / 11.50
505	Int. Class	5.05 / 1.96 / 16.30
Flying Fifteen	Nat. Class	5.80 / 1.88 / 17.00
Tempest	Int. Class	6.68 / 1.90 / 22.90
Squib	Nat. Class	7.17 / 1.94 / 22.00
Sonata	Nat. Class	7.75 / 2.15 – 2.50 / 20.00
Dragon	Int. Class	8.90 / 1.97 / 26.60

The diagrams on p.26 contain figures which, reading from top to bottom, are length, breadth and sail area.

published, and the designs and method of construction must be defined. Also a minimum number of boats must belong to the class association.

The most popular classes are naturally the six **Olympic Classes** which are taken from the International Classes. The following six boats belong to these: Finn-dinghy, 470, F.D., Tornado, Star, Soling. In 1984 the windglider will become the seventh 'boat'.

Sail Symbols

The different types of boats have the class symbol on the mainsail e.g. a motif, the letters F.D., numbers 470, etc. Underneath this symbol there is a number which is the registration number in that country's sailing union. In front of the number there is also a letter showing the nationality, e.g.

B	Belgium	KA	Australia
BL	Brazil	KC	Canada
D	Denmark	KZ	New Zealand
E	Spain	L	Finland
F	France	M	Hungary
G	West Germany	N	Norway
GO	East Germany	OE	Austria
GR	Greece	PZ	Poland
H	Holland	S	Sweden
I	Italy	SR	USSR
IR	Ireland	US	USA
IS	Israel	Y	Yugoslavia
K	Great Britain	Z	Switzerland

Usually the sailmaker will also add his own symbol and this is normally found in the region of the tack or clew. Oddly enough, the class symbol, number and nationality signs are placed higher on the starboard side than on the port side!

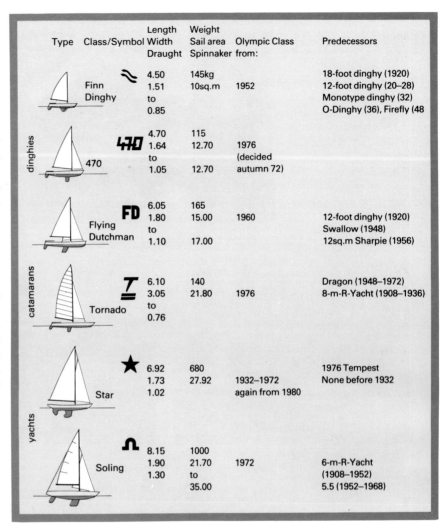

Type	Class/Symbol		Length Width Draught	Weight Sail area Spinnaker	Olympic Class from:	Predecessors
dinghies	Finn Dinghy	≋	4.50 1.51 to 0.85	145kg 10sq.m	1952	18-foot dinghy (1920) 12-foot dinghy (20–28) Monotype dinghy (32) O-Dinghy (36), Firefly (48
	470	470	4.70 1.64 to 1.05	115 12.70 12.70	1976 (decided autumn 72)	
	Flying Dutchman	FD	6.05 1.80 to 1.10	165 15.00 17.00	1960	12-foot dinghy (1920) Swallow (1948) 12sq.m Sharpie (1956)
catamarans	Tornado	𝕋	6.10 3.05 to 0.76	140 21.80	1976	Dragon (1948–1972) 8-m-R-Yacht (1908–1936)
yachts	Star	★	6.92 1.73 1.02	680 27.92	1932–1972 again from 1980	1976 Tempest None before 1932
	Soling	∩	8.15 1.90 1.30	1000 21.70 to 35.00	1972	6-m-R-Yacht (1908–1952) 5.5 (1952–1968)

Olympic Classes

Olympic Classes (1984)

1 Finn-Dinghy
2 470

3 Flying Dutchman
4 Tornado

5 Star
6 Soling

28

Ropes

Terminology — Material — Manufacture

In sailing language the main length of a rope is called the **standing part** and the short end the **free** or **bitter end**. A thin rope is called **twine** or **cord**, and a thick rope is called a **hawser**. Rope is made from:
- **Natural materials** (e.g. hemp and sisal) — very rarely used today.
- **Man-made materials**
  a) Nylon
  b) Polyester (e.g. Dacron, terylene)
  c) Polyethylene and polypropylene
  d) Kevlar (very new)
- **Steel wire** which was formerly galvanised steel, but is now invariably stainless steel (known by the symbols V2A and V4A).

Modern synthetic ropes have many advantages over the old-fashioned ropes; for instance, they do not rot and are two to three times stronger.

A distinction is made between **laid** and **plaited** ropes. Laid rope is very strong and easy to splice. It is made from threads wound into yarn. This is twist-ed into strands (ply) which are then twisted into the final rope. Three- or four-ply rope is common. A four-ply rope can also be made by wrapping the four plies round a single strand called the *core*.

If the twist is to the right it is called a Z-twist, or left-hand lay, and if to the left it is an S-twist, or right-hand lay.

To make a rope the threads are first twisted to the right to produce the yarn. This is then twisted to the left to make the strands which are finally twisted once more to the right.

- Polyester is especially suitable for sheets, a plaited rope being preferred because of its suppleness.
- Laid nylon rope is best for making up lines, anchor ropes and tow ropes because of its strength and elasticity.

Polyethylene and polypropylene ropes are less popular with sailors since they tend to be very inflexible.

Halyards are usually made from one part flexible wire rope and one part rope. The first section of the halyard, which is wire, reaches from the mast

1 & 2: 16-strand plaited rope (10mm); 3: 8-strand plaited rope (8mm);
4: laid rope (10mm); 5: laid rope (16mm, 3-ply);
a, b, c: strands (plies); b: strand made from threads twisted into yarn.

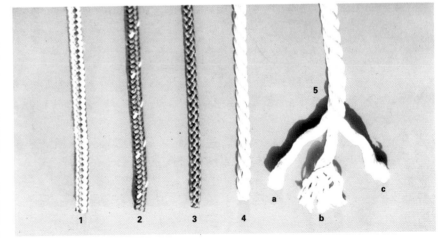

Whipping

Eye splice

Laid rope can be easily and strongly joined by twisting together the individual strands. This is called *splicing*. The most commonly used splice is the **eye splice** which produces an eye at the end of a rope.

Knots

Nautical knots must have three properties:
- They must be simple and quick to tie.
- They must hold (pull tight under pressure).
- They should be easily untied when not under pressure.

head to the belaying cleat (or hook) when the sail is set. It does not stretch but holds the sail well in position. The rope section, however, is more pleasant to handle.

Whipping and Splicing

Each rope on board must be prevented from fraying by whipping, and every aspiring sailor should be able to manage at least a makeshift whipping. For this he will need whipping yarn and a knife. Synthetic ropes are very easy to whip, since the ends need only be held over a flame to seal them.

Splicing the ends of a synthetic rope

Three important concepts to do with knots are *bight*, *eye* and *turn*. A hairpin-type loop in a rope is called a **bight**. An **eye** is a completed loop, and a **turn** is when the rope is wrapped round an object (i.e. a bitt). The following knots are basic to every sailor:

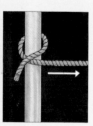

Bight   Eye   Turn

Belaying a cleat   Cleat belayed with
Right   Wrong   slippery hitch

Figure of Eight Knot

Prevents a rope from slipping out of a block or fairlead. Used e.g. on sheets.

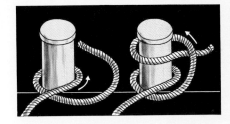

Clove Hitch

Used to fasten ropes to bits or spars. Since it only holds under pressure, it should be secured with two half hitches.

Rolling Hitch

Used for tying a thin rope to a thick one, the latter being under tension. Used for securing the tail of a handy-billy or snatch block to a larger rope, or for tying a painter to a thicker tow rope.

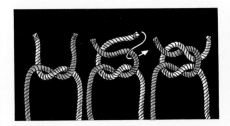

Reef Knot

To tie ropes of equal thickness, e.g. reefing lines when used the old-fashioned reef points.

Simple and Double Sheetbend

Used to tie ends of different thicknesses together, e.g. fastening the painter to a tow rope with or without eyes, lengthening an anchor cable.

Slippery Hitch

Used in situations where speed of untying is vital, e.g. to belay the tow rope on the mast, to belay a sheet at top speed, to belay a halyard.

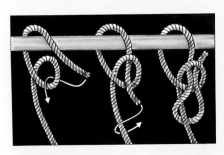

Simple Bowline

This knot forms an eye which does not slip, e.g. when fastening up to a bollard or ring. It will hold well under continual tightening and slackening conditions.

Round Turn with Two Half Hitches

Used for tying up to a cross beam or similar, e.g. securing a tow rope to the mast.

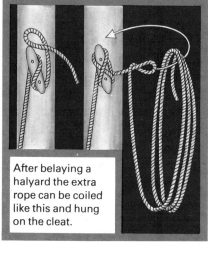

After belaying a halyard the extra rope can be coiled like this and hung on the cleat.

After belaying a halyard the extra rope should be tidily coiled up and cleated between the mast and the part of the halyard under tension. Another possibility would be to pull the last loop through from behind, and then twist and hang it over the cleat.

Note: If this is not properly done, you may find that when lowering the sail you are unable to untie the halyard fast enough and the whole lot will disappear upwards!

Belaying and Coiling

To **belay** a line (e.g. a halyard) to a cleat, we first of all make a round turn, making sure the line will come free when pulled. The line is then fastened around the cleat in a figure of eight, the final turn being twisted to hold it fast. A slippery hitch in the last turn makes it very easy to untie (with one pull).

You should always avoid leaving rope lying around. It should be *coiled* up tidily. When doing this try to make sure that the loops are the same size, and add a few turns round the middle of the coils. The last turn can be made into a loop, pushed through the upper part of the coil and pulled over the top (see series of photographs above).

The Care of Your Boat

Maintenance

A well-maintained boat will not only look good but will withstand wear and tear more easily, and will enjoy a much longer life.

- After every sailing day you must clean the deck, cockpit and sides of your boat. You will need a bucket and cleaning cloths.
- Plastic tubes may be placed over the shrouds to minimise chafing, especially the Genoa and jibsheet and mainsail shrouds.
- If the mainsail rubs on the spreader, small rubber balls can be used as protection.
- Mooring lines undergo a great deal of wear and tear in the fairleads; it is a good idea to protect them with rubber tubing or cloths.
- Always use fenders to protect the side of the boat.
- In a strong wind the constant banging of the halyards on a boat in harbour or moored to a jetty makes a disagreeable noise, and can also damage the mast. The halyards should be lashed to the shroud with shock cord or ties.
- One of the worst things a sailor can do is to leave a boat over a long period tied up to a buoy, jetty or on the beach with slack sheets and flapping sail. The threads of the cloth, the 'finish' of the cloth and the stitches will certainly be damaged — much more than when sailing in heavy weather. The batten pockets may also become torn. A careful sailor will always take in his sail after tying up, and fold it if he is going to be a while.
- Scratches and grazes on fibreglass boats must be repaired straight away since the laminate will take in water, and in winter it will suffer frost damage.
- Ropes which have come into contact with chemicals must be washed immediately. Always replace worn ropes.

Winter Storage

To prepare the boat for winter storage:
- First of all remove the boat from the water and clean the bottom.
- Remove the rigging (de-rig) and everything else which could be affected by frost or could rot.
- Remove the floor boards or tip them up. Open all drawers, storage areas, hatches and doors to let the air circulate.
- Dry any wet patches.
- If you have an engine you should take a quick glance at the working parts. If it has been in salt water it must be thoroughly rinsed with fresh water and treated with a preservative.
- Remove the battery and store it away so that it cannot be damaged. Grease the poles and store in a dry, frost-free place. Charge every eight weeks.
- The engine block should be drained of all water and given a corrosion protection treatment to prevent frost damage.

Wintering the boats at a sailing school. The boats at the back of the photograph are tied to the slipway, ready to be taken out of the water. The dinghy (front, left) is being de-rigged, while the people on the right are cleaning and drying.

A yacht pulled out of the water. It is important to support and protect the ballasted keel and prop (shore up) long overhangs.

after wooden boat will only require a rub down and one coat of paint. If the boat is not in such good condition, several coats will be required after the old paint has been removed by paint stripper, rubbing down or blow torch.

■ Remember never to use a scraper on a steel or glassfibre boat, and never burn paint off a glassfibre boat.

■ The cleaning materials used on synthetic boats should not contain any strong organic solvents or abrasives.

■ If possible the boat should be stored in a sheltered place. A yacht must be carefully supported by wooden scaffolding so there is no possibility of it tipping over. It is important to ensure the keel fin is especially well protected.

■ If a small yacht has to be over-wintered outdoors under a tarpaulin you must ensure that no water is either in the boat to start with or can get into the boat and cause frost damage.

■ The mast is laid flat — not sagging in the middle. It is a good idea to take the opportunity to check the standing rigging for wear and tear.

Spring Overhaul

Work to be carried out in the spring:
■ Synthetic boats do not need a lot of maintenance, in fact they do not usually require a spring coat of paint unless, of course, you want to change the colour. If your boat is going to be moored in the water it is a good idea to give the underwater hull a coat of anti-fouling paint.

■ When varnishing a wooden boat in spring you must make sure you do it on a wind-free day or in a dust-free room, never in direct sunlight or damp conditions.

■ Always follow the manufacturer's instructions when varnishing. Yacht varnish has to be carefully handled — there is a danger of certain types actually heating up and self-igniting if left lying around in the pot. Never mix different types of varnish or paint one type on top of another; the old undercoat could be damaged or the varnish may simply fail to hold.

■ A bonded wood laminate boat in good condition need not be varnished every year. A well looked-

3 Sailing Theory

Directions

Directions Relating to the Boat

There are several expressions used on board for the sake of complete clarity.

- The right side of the boat is called the **starboard** (SB).
- The left side of the boat is called the **port** (P).

The words *right* and *left* are never used since they depend for their sense on the direction in which you are looking and are therefore ambiguous (e.g. when sailing astern). With starboard and port you always know which direction is meant no matter where you are standing or in what direction you are travelling.

- The front part of the boat (**fore**) is called the **bow**.
- The back part of the boat (**aft**) is called the **stern**.

While the expressions *fore* and *aft* denote places actually on the boat, the following are expressions used to indicate points outside the boat:

- **Ahead** denotes an area outside the boat in front of its cross axis.
- **Astern** is the area directly behind the boat.
- **Starboard and port bow** are areas to the front and side of the boat.
- **Port quarter and starboard quarter** are areas to the back and side of the boat.
- **Port beam and starboard beam** are areas directly to the side of the boat.

The term *clear* is used to denote exactness when referring to directions, i.e.:

- **Clear ahead** means exactly to the front of, and
- **Clear astern** means exactly behind.

Also remember:

If the boom is over the starboard side you will be sailing on a **port tack**. And similarly, you will be on a **starboard tack** when the boom is over the port side. It is important always to know

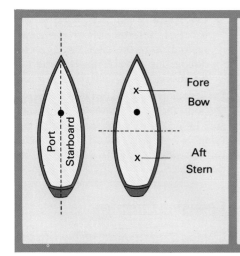

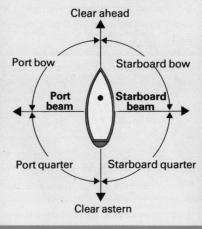

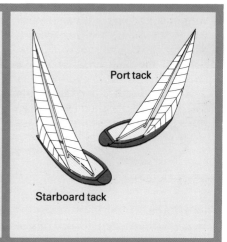

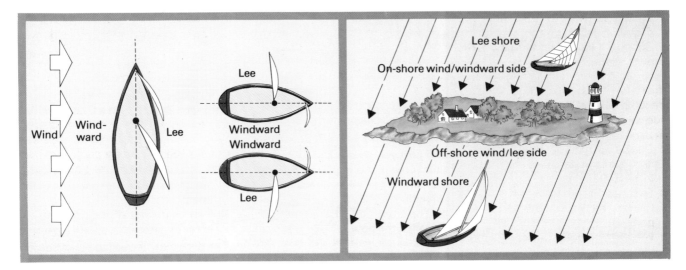

which tack you are on because of the right of way regulations (see p.103).

Directions Relating to the Wind

Every sailor should know these directions thoroughly:

■ **Windward** is the side facing the wind.
■ **Lee** is the side away from the wind.

The expressions windward and lee are used not only in conjunction with the boat but also with other objects, e.g. jetty, tree, island.

Note: The concepts windward and lee when used in connection with the coastline can lead to confusion! Each island, it is true, has a windward and a lee side. The coastline itself, however, is described according to the position of the boat: i.e.:

■ **Windward shore** is the coast lying to windward of the boat. It is on the lee side of the island, and the wind is **off-shore**.
■ **Lee shore** is the coast lying to leeward of the boat. It is on the windward side of the island and can be dangerous for yachts. The wind is **on-shore**.

On a sailing boat the lee side is always the side the boom is on, the windward side being the opposite one. Even if the wind is coming directly from behind the lee side is still the side where the boom is!

Changing Direction

Changing direction in relation to the wind (changing course) is called:

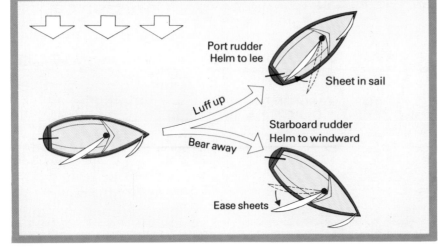

- **Luffing up** when the bow turns into the wind, and
- **Bearing away** when the bow turns away from the wind.

The *rudder* is used to change direction, the boat always turning towards the side on which the rudder blade is positioned. We talk of:
- **Starboard rudder** when the rudder is on the starboard side and the boat turns to starboard.
- **Port rudder** when the rudder is on the port side and the boat turns to port.
- **Windward rudder** when the boat has a tendency to luff up.
- **Lee rudder** when the boat has a tendency to bear away.

The first two expressions are used as commands, and always describe the position of the rudder, not the tiller.

Other important points to remember: When you alter course you will usually have to adjust the set of your sail (unless you are simply dealing with a change of wind direction), so that the angle of the sail to the wind is kept at the most efficient. To do this the sheets are used:
- **Sheet in** the sail when luffing up.
- **Ease** the sheet when bearing away.

Courses to the Wind

The direction in which a boat travels is its *course*. A course can be steered using a compass, e.g. on cruising yachts to help sail towards a predetermined goal. You can also take your course

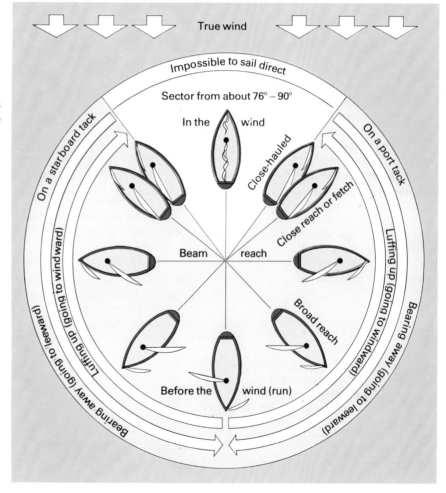

(and this is very often the case) from the wind.

The concept of courses in relation to the wind is extremely important and it is one of the first things a sailing student must learn. The diagram shows a sector from about 76° – 90° in which it is impossible to sail. On this course a boat will soon be brought to a standstill with sail flapping, and may even be driven backwards:
■ The boat is lying **in irons**.
Forward movement is, therefore, only possible from an angle of 38° – 45° (depending on the type of boat) to the true wind. We call this a:
■ **Close-hauled course.**

On this course you will be pointing the boat as high as possible to the wind. The sails must be completely sheeted in. On a close-hauled course, when the boat is pointing as high as possible to the wind so that the front edge of the sail immediately begins to lift at the slightest luffing up, you are said to be sailing **hard on the wind**. On this course, the boat will be pointing somewhat higher than on a close-hauled course, but it will lose speed, so usually there is little to be gained.

Other courses:
■ **Close reach:** Sailing freer than close hauled — the wind blows from the side at an angle of 90°.
■ **Broad reach:** The wind blows more astern than on a reach course.
■ **Before the wind (run):** The wind blows exactly from behind (from *clear astern*).
All these courses can be sailed on a starboard or port tack.

> **Note:** The further a course is from the wind, the more you must ease the sheets.

A course may only be steered by reference to a static object, a clear reading on the compass or a stable wind direction. It is therefore only possible to steer a course by the **true wind** and not by the *apparent wind* (see next chapter), which is constantly changing when the boat changes speed or the wind is gusting. Several sailing textbooks completely ignore this fact and advocate setting courses by the apparent wind, which inevitably leads to the following absurd situation:

Imagine two boats sailing exactly parallel to each other in the same direction but at different speeds. One boat is very fast and the apparent wind is blowing from diagonally in front; the other boat is much slower and the apparent wind is blowing from the side. We would have to say that the faster boat is sailing *close-hauled* and the slower boat is on a *reach*! This is, of course, absurd.

> **Note:** We take our course from the true wind, remembering that the angle of the apparent wind can vary according to the boat's speed.

True Wind — Apparent Wind

Whenever a boat is moving forward there is always an **apparent wind**. It is this wind which works on the moving boat, propelling it forward, and it is therefore impossible to sail without knowing how it works. What is the apparent wind? On a motionless boat, e.g. at anchor, or tied to a buoy or a jetty, you take the wind from the direction it is blowing from. This, then, is the **true wind**. The wind you feel on a motorboat travelling at speed is the **wind of the boat's own speed**. This wind is always exactly opposite to the direction of travel and its speed matches that of the boat.

The apparent wind, which is of vital importance to sailors, is a combination of the wind of the boat's own speed and the true wind calculated by vector addition.

The arrow heads denote the direction of the wind and the shafts give a measurement of the wind speed.

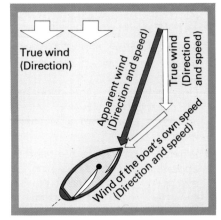

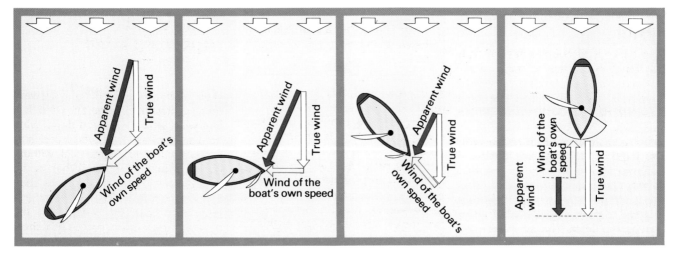

The following rules are applicable to the apparent wind:

■ As long as the boat is moving, the true wind and the apparent wind can never be the same.

■ When a boat is moving the strength and direction of the true wind cannot be measured exactly.

■ The apparent wind always blows more from the front than the true wind. Only on a downwind course does it retain the same direction.

■ When sailing close-hauled the apparent wind is noticeably stronger than the true wind; however, it is blowing from an unfavourable angle and only a small part of it is instrumental in propelling the boat forward.

■ On a reach course the influence of the apparent wind is advantageous since it comes from a favourable angle.

■ When sailing before the wind the apparent wind is always less than the true wind. The faster the boat sails the smaller the apparent wind becomes. (On this course it is easy

to underestimate the strength of the true wind!)

On a moving boat the wind vane (the burgee or racing pennant at the top of the mast) shows only the direction of the apparent wind. Therefore, if you want to come into a jetty using the true wind (see p.77), e.g. in order to moor the boat on the lee side, you must **not** look at the wind vane to find out the direction of the true wind. You can take the direction from the wind vane on a stationary boat, or a flag on land, smoke from a chimney etc.

It is also important to know that the apparent wind can change, altering the direction of the wind vane, without the true wind changing at all! This can happen if there is a squall. The speed of the true wind will suddenly increase while the wind of the boat's own speed remains constant. As a result, the apparent wind will alter towards the true wind; it **veers aft**. The boat will increase its speed, i.e. the velocity of the wind of movement will increase

The apparent wind changing according to the course.

(while the speed of the true wind remains increased). The apparent wind will now move towards the boat's direction. When the gust is over the velocity of the true wind returns to what it was originally, while the wind of the boat's own speed remains increased. The apparent wind is now even more strongly influenced by the boat's speed than at the beginning of the gust, until the wind of the boat's own speed has subsided again.

Use can be made of a squall by luffing up and then bearing away at just the right moment.

> **Note:** *Veers aft* means that the wind changes direction and blows more astern, and is therefore more favourable.

Why you can sail

Propulsion through Resistance

When sailing *before the wind* (i.e. when the wind is blowing from behind — astern), the force moving the boat forward is produced because the slack sail is offering a resistance to the wind. The sail traps (blocks) the wind, which moves the boat. The air stream will break up and form turbulent zones in the lee of the sail.

Therefore the larger the sail surface the better. All that is needed is for the sail to *trap* a certain quantity of air for the boat to move forward. The best sails for this purpose are those cut to bulge out in the wind. It is for this reason that spinnakers have a parachute-like shape.

Propulsion by Lift

The propulsion derived from sailing on a broad reach or a close-hauled course is, however, different. The wind is no longer trapped by the sail at about 10° – 20° to the apparent wind, but deflected from its normal course. The air then flows round the sail to windward and leeward at different speeds. The windward current is trapped a little by the sail, resulting in a slightly raised pressure. At the same time the faster lee current forms a low pressure area. In this way unequal forces are built up on either side of the sail. If we combine these different pressures we get a resulting total force called the *wind*

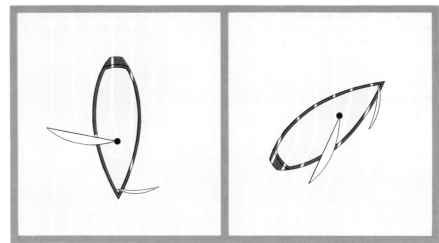

Left: Propulsion by resistance. On a downwind course the air is trapped, resulting in forwards movement. Right: Propulsion by deflection of the apparent wind. The air currents hug either side of the sail without breaking up (laminar currents). This is also called sailing in the 'range of lift'.

pressure or *sailing thrust* whose point of attack we can imagine as being at the sail's centre of effort. This wind pressure acts at right angles to the chord across the curve of the sail (roughly in the area of the boom).

If we draw in the wind pressure on a sketch of a boat sailing close-hauled we can immediately see that it is not in the same direction as that in which the boat is moving. In order to find the part of the wind pressure which moves the

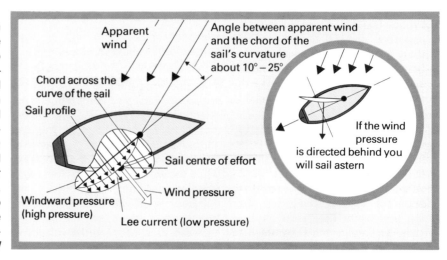

boat forward, we have to divide it into two parts:

■ 1. That which is parallel to the boat's long axis and pointing forward. This *force of propulsion* results in a forwards movement,

■ 2. That which is at right angles to the boat's long axis. Since it is tending to try to force the boat at 90° to the direction in which it is travelling (making leeway), it is called the *transverse* or *lateral force*.

The result of these forces is surprising: the advantageous forward-directed *propulsion force* is small, whereas the disadvantageous *transverse force* is much larger. The fact that, in spite of this, you can still travel forward is due to the well-designed shape of the boat. It offers little resistance to the water along its long axis, but seen from the side it has a relatively large surface of resistance under water (the lateral plane). The transverse force, therefore, finds it very difficult to push the boat against the lateral plane's resistance.

Making Leeway and Heeling

The outcome of the 'battle' between the transverse force and the lateral plane is a tendency to *make leeway*, which cannot be avoided and which makes itself felt much more strongly when sailing close-hauled. The further you bear away, the smaller the effect of the transverse force and the less leeway you will make. As well as making leeway, the boat will also *heel* (tilt to the side).

Making leeway and heeling have the following relationship to each other:

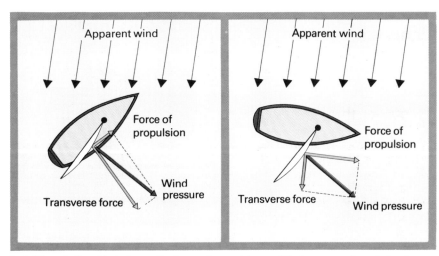

Left: The relationship between the force of propulsion and the transverse force is least favourable on a close-hauled course. Right: On a reach and part of a broad reach course the propulsion force is much larger. Sailing boats reach their highest speeds on these courses.

■ For example, a dinghy with a raised centre-board making leeway will heel less. However, when a boat is heeling it will also make more leeway.

In practice this fact can be made use of when, for instance, trying to sail the boat upright in a suitable wind. In a strong wind you should raise the centre-board a little if you feel there is a danger of capsizing, thereby intentionally increasing your leeway to reduce the heeling.

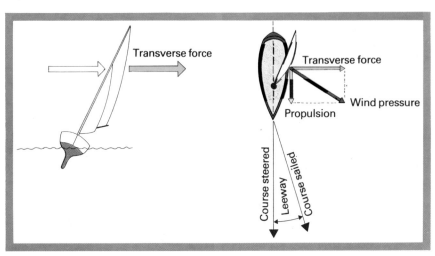

Stability

The stability (transverse stability) of a sailing boat (the ability to right itself after heeling) differs a great deal between dinghies and yachts. Stability is achieved:

■ By means of the hull shape (form stability), and

■ By means of weight or the position of the centre of gravity.

On a yacht the weight centre of gravity, determined by the low-ballasted keel, lies below the water-line and below the form centre of gravity (the centre of uplift); stability is achieved in the first place by **weight**. The result is that the more a yacht tilts over to the side (*heels*) the more the righting effect is brought into play. It is therefore very stable and will not capsize. It is comforting to know that you cannot capsize, but do remember that a yacht can sink (if it has not been fitted with appropriate buoyancy) if, for example, it is placed on its side and fills with water.

Dinghies have no ballast (the weight centre of gravity lies above the form centre of gravity); their stability (form stability) is produced because of their relatively wide hulls. The result is that initially form stability is relatively good, but when heeling strongly it very quickly decreases and a capsize is possible. The crew can move the weight centre of gravity to windward by sitting out or using the trapeze, and in this way increase the boat's righting ability. If a dinghy is equipped with suitable buoyancy aids (air tanks, air tubes, poly styrene blocks) it will have very little water in the cockpit after capsizing and can usually be righted quickly and sailed on.

Section of boat with good form stability (dinghy)

Section of boat with good weight stability (yacht)

The weight centre of gravity (W) of dinghies and dinghy cruisers lies above the form centre of gravity (F)

The weight centre of gravity (W) of yachts lies below the form centre of gravity (F)

Weight and form stability:
W — Weight centre of gravity, F — Lift or form centre of gravity, L — lever, which gives a measurement for the righting moment.
On a dinghy (boats 1 and 3) a decrease in stability is clearly seen when it heels. When a yacht heels, however, (boats 2 and 4) stability increases. On dinghy no. 5 the weight centre of gravity has been shifted to windward by the crew sitting out and using the trapeze which has increased the righting moment (compare with dinghy 3).

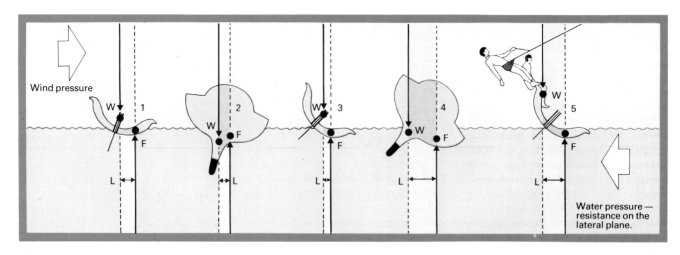

Wind pressure

Water pressure — resistance on the lateral plane.

Carrying Lee and Weather Helm

A sailing boat will only reach its maximum speed if it is correctly balanced. If the balance is not right it will show a tendency either to turn into the wind i.e. luff to windward, or to turn away from the wind i.e. bear away to leeward. This is called *carrying weather helm* or *carrying lee helm*. If the helmsman gets himself into this position he will constantly have to be correcting his course by using the rudder, which will slow the boat down.

How does this happen?

In the section on *Propulsion by Lift* we discussed the *wind pressure* which is made up of many parts, and if we imagine all the forces concentrated on one spot, this would be the **centre of effort** (CE). In the same way all the forces of the water are acting on the hull, producing a total pressure called *hydro dynamic pressure* which acts on the **centre of lateral resistance**. This centre of lateral resistance (CLR) lies on the centre of gravity of the lateral surface, i.e. near the keel fin on keelboats and close to the centre-board on dinghies. If the wind pressure and the hydrodynamic pressure are in line (the centre of effort is a little forward of the centre of lateral resistance) the boat is balanced — carrying neither lee nor weather helm. If the wind pressure is behind the hydrodynamic pressure (the centre of effort is in line with the centre of lateral resistance or even behind it) the boat will carry weather

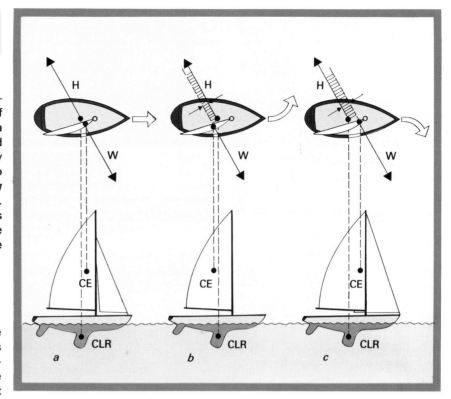

Basic principle of lee and weather helm:
a The centre of effort (CE) lies a little in front of the centre of lateral resistance (CLR) enabling the hydrodynamic pressure of the hull (H) and aerodynamic pressure of the sails (wind pressure — W) to work in one line; the boat has good course stability.
b The centre of effort lies behind the centre of lateral resistance, the wind pressure lying behind the hydrodynamic hull pressure. This results in a turning moment with the boat carrying weather helm.
c The centre of effort lies far forward of the centre of lateral resistance. The wind pressure is therefore too far forward of the hydrodynamic pressure and results in a turning moment with the boat carrying lee helm.

helm. On the other hand if the wind pressure is in front of the hydrodynamic pressure (the centre of effort is too far forward of the centre of lateral resistance) the boat will carry lee helm (see diagrams). Strong heeling encourages weather helm, since the centre of effort wanders far out from amidships and the propulsion has to work on a larger lever.

> **Tip:** In strong winds sail the boat upright, and raise some of the centre board to bring the lateral resistance aft.

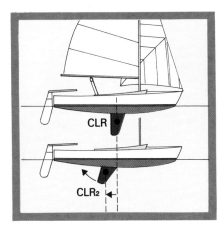

On a dinghy with a pivoting centre-board the centre of lateral resistance (CLR) can be moved aft (CLR2) by raising the centre-board)

Correcting Lee and Weather Helm

In the first place the position and rake of the mast are largely responsible for the balance of a boat. There are also other ways of achieving or preventing lee or weather helm. To summarise:

1. **Weather helm** can be avoided by:
- Tilting the mast forward.
- Enlarging the jib.
- Reefing or flattening the mainsail.
- Moving traveller to lee — flatten mainsail (centre of effort moves forward).
- Moving the centre of lateral resistance aft (crew moves aft, centre-board raised a little. Remember: a fixed centre-board can have the opposite effect!).
2. **Lee helm** (opposite to no. 1) can be avoided by:
- Moving or tilting mast aft.
- Using smaller jib.
- Enlarging the mainsail.
- Moving traveller from lee to centre.
- Moving centre of lateral resistance forward (crew forward).

Remember: You can alter the centre of lateral resistance by raising or lowering the rudder (raise — centre of lateral resistance moves aft; lower — centre of lateral resistance moves forward). This, however, is unrealistic in practice since a rudder blade should always be well down in the water (see also *Sailing Practice*). It is possible to move the centre of effort by making the mainsail or jib lift (if the jib lifts, the boat will carry weather helm; if the mainsail lifts, the boat will carry lee helm). Since one would not normally sail with a lifting sail, this is impractical. However, it could be useful for short term measures, such as when initiating a manoeuvre or if you have to steer without a rudder (let the jib lift and you will luff up, let the mainsail lift and haul in the jib and you will bear away).

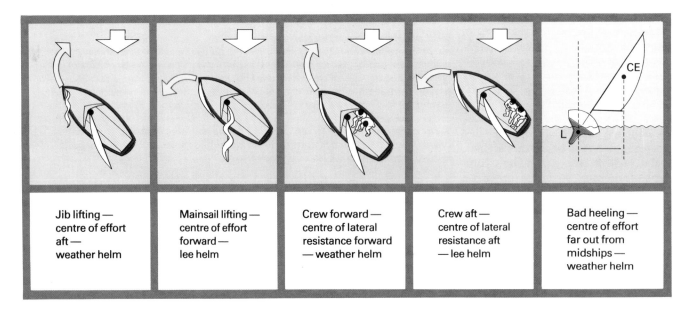

| Jib lifting — centre of effort aft — weather helm | Mainsail lifting — centre of effort forward — lee helm | Crew forward — centre of lateral resistance forward — weather helm | Crew aft — centre of lateral resistance aft — lee helm | Bad heeling — centre of effort far out from midships — weather helm |

Planing

A displacement boat cannot move faster than the bow and stern waves it creates and there is a certain speed, called the **critical speed** (upper limit), which it is impossible for the boat to exceed. The highest possible speed is reached when the hull lies in a valley between the bow wave and the stern wave. This critical speed depends on the length of the water-line, and can be calculated by using the following formula:
Speed in km/h = $\sqrt{\text{water-line length (in metres)}} \times 4.5$.

For example, a yacht with a water-line length of 9m would reach a speed of 13.5km/h = 7.3 knots. A boat cannot, therefore, go faster than its critical speed under its own steam. This barrier, however, can be forcibly overcome if the boat, for example, is towed too fast by a larger vessel. The stresses on the hull would be enormous and the yacht would suffer serious damage.

On the other hand *planing boats* (light boats with flat bottoms, wider aft) can generate additional dynamic lift, and can ride up and sit on their own bow waves, leaving their stern waves behind. In this way they can exceed the critical speed by **planing**. The further the stern wave is left behind, the faster the planing. The bow lifts out of the water, reducing the immersed surface of the hull, so underwater resistance is greatly reduced. Remarkable speeds can be achieved when planing.

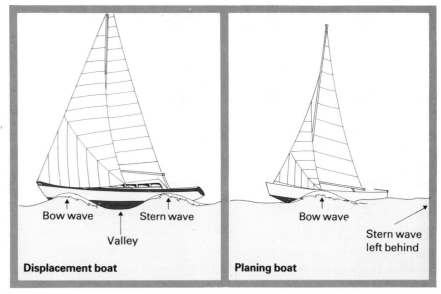

Bow wave   Stern wave

Valley

Displacement boat

Bow wave

Stern wave left behind

Planing boat

A heavier boat may exceed its critical speed for short periods only by **surfing**, which is not to be confused with planing. It is achieved by riding up the waves and dropping into the valleys.

A planing Laser dinghy

31262
SASIE

4　Sailing Practice

Safety — Health

Before we embark upon the practical aspects of sailing, one very important sentence: 'Look after your health and always bear safety in mind!'.

This also means that you must never underestimate wind and weather. You must always have one **buoyancy jacket** per person on board (even in the calmest weather!). Should these be B.S.I. Kitemarked life-jackets? In our

This strong wind definitely requires a life-jacket. This one has a collar.

Dinghy buoyancy aid without collar. No excuses that it is uncomfortable!

A 'sailing offence': bare feet! Apart from the danger of slipping off we can clearly see that the girl's feet must be hurting her.

Not a good idea to wear a bikini. Also sitting on the side of a small sporty boat like this (Laser) will soon become painful.

Good foul-weather gear: the overall. The best colours are yellow, red or orange.

opinion: yes and no! 'Yes' when sailing a yacht and, of course, when cruising. 'No' in dinghies on inshore or inland waters where a buoyancy aid should be comfortable. The reason for this is that B.S.I. non-inflatable jackets have large collars which can lead to all sorts of problems (inflatable jackets are not at all suitable for dinghy sailing). For example, the collar could get caught up in the sheets, sheet fittings or boom and cause a capsize, or you could delay putting on your life-jacket, because it is uncomfortable, or even leave it off altogether; this, of course, is very dangerous.

A sailor should always wear **shoes** with non-slip soles. Sailing barefoot is dangerous: you can easily slip on a wet boat and at the very least injure your toes. And the shoreline is littered with rocks and glass.

Sailing in **swimwear** in calm weather can be most enjoyable, but is dangerous when there is a wind. The body can quickly cool down, the back muscles stiffen up in the cold draught and your reactions will begin to slow down over a period of time. You can also give yourself a nasty knock and bare knees will always tire quickly. So wear long trousers (jeans) or Bermuda shorts, which will at least protect the pressure points on the back of the thighs when sitting out, and a T-shirt.

On cool days, in rain or wind when the spray is flying, it is essential to wear a **foul-weather suit**. Apart from a sweater this consists of an 'oilskin', or waterproof overall, boots with slip-proof soles and, if necessary, a sou'wester. If you are racing you might use a neoprene wet suit instead.

Mooring

Light planing dinghies are always kept on shore when not in use. With the help of a small *slipway* they can be put in the water very easily. The two-man Star yacht is always removed from the water by means of a hoist.

Other boats are tied up to a buoy or jetty.

■ A boat is normally moored to a buoy by means of the forelines (bowline). Remember: feed the lines through the fairlead on the bow and leave enough length so that the buoy does not bang against the sides of the boat. If the boat is going to be left for some time it is better to pull the buoy on board and to belay the buoy chains direct to the bow.

■ When tying up to a jetty you can either moor your boat alongside the jetty or between bollards in a box (see diagram).

The centre-board on a dinghy is always raised. The rudder equipment is lifted

Boats A and B moored in the box, tied with two bowlines and two sternlines.
Boat B's sternlines are crossed to give a better tension angle. The lines must have enough play to allow the boat a little movement and to prevent it from 'hanging' on the lines. Boat C is lying alongside the quay and as well as bow and sternlines it also has a forespring and aftspring to prevent the boat from swinging to and fro. The fenders are vital here!

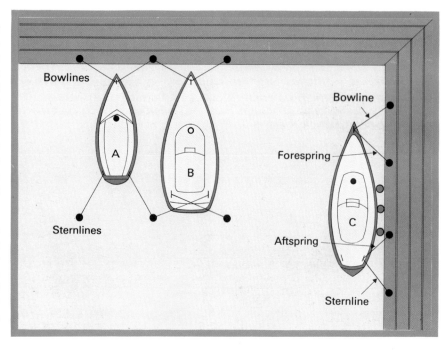

Bowlines

Bowline

Forespring

A

B

Sternlines

C

Aftspring

Sternline

boom with the mainsheet (see series of photographs p.52). If the boat is to be moored for a longer time or if rain is expected you should cover the folded mainsail with a sail cover. In strong winds it is best to unshackle the jib altogether and put it below deck, or at least lower it into the boat with the tack still shackled. Always raise the centre-board and rudder every time you leave the boat. If the centre-board is left lowered, the case could well be damaged by continuous bumping when the boat rolls. It will also have a detrimental effect on the swinging of the boat at anchor or when it is moored to a buoy or on the lee side of a jetty. It will be hampered when swinging round into the wind and in a storm could even capsize. A lowered rudder and an unfastened tiller could be damaged by continuous bumping.

Moorings in a harbour: the boats (Pirates here) are lying bow towards jetty, and the sterns are tied with two sternlines to the bollards. The raised centre-board and rudder and the secured tiller can be seen on the boats on the left.
1 For larger boats the typical mooring knot is the bowline.
2 For smaller boats the clove hitch may be used.
3 The clove hitch is made secure by means of two half hitches, and if there is extra line,
4 The tidy sailor will throw a loop over the bollard before making the two half hitches, so the line does not dangle in the water.

out or the rudder blade raised. To prevent the cockpit from filling with water when it rains, open boats at least should be entirely covered with a cockpit cover. When folding the cover make sure that the outside remains outside!

The sails should never be left hoisted even if the boat is going to be moored for a short time only, e.g. if you are going for a coffee break. It is also not enough simply to take in the sails. They should be folded, making the mainsail into a sort of pocket, and tied to the

After a day on the water you should *clean and secure the ship*: even the boards should be taken up (as far as possible). The mainsail should be made up on top of the boom, and good racing sails should be taken in and folded up (see series of photographs on p.53).

1   2   3   4

Preparing the Boat to Sail

A boat is prepared for sailing as follows:
- Cockpit cover is removed and neatly folded, remembering to keep the outside to the outside.
- If the dinghy is moored in the water the next thing to do is lower the centre-board (as far as it will go depending on the water depth) so that you do not forget to do it later when casting off!
- Check standing and running rigging and if necessary pump out water.
- Take on board essential equipment such as paddles, life-jackets, etc.
- Remove mainsail from bag and place the foot, clew first, into the groove of the boom, from the mast end.
- Secure the tack first (different fittings depending on type of boat: seizing, hooks, peg, pin or shackle).
- Pull foot taut so that there are no vertical creases and then attach the clew to the boom end with seizing.
- The exact adjustment of the foot tension depends on the wind strength (see *Trimming*).
- Before shackling the sail head to the main halyard make sure that neither halyard nor sail are twisted — otherwise you will be in for some unpleasant surprises when you hoist the sail!
- After shackling the sail head feed the luff line into the mast groove (some larger boats have sliders with a track for this purpose) and pull up the sail a little (up to half a metre) ready to hoist.
- Do not forget to put the battens in the batten pockets.

1 If the mainsail tack is fastened with seizing, thread it through the sail eye several times, pull tight and secure with reef knots.

2 When securing the mainsail clew using seizing, remember to wrap it round the boom.

3 On this 470 the upper blocks of the central pulley system are shackled direct on the boom and run on a small track.

4 Older types of boat often have a reefing claw (here two rings) for the upper block. The advantage is that the boom can be turned inside the ring, and if necessary the sail can be reefed by the roll reef method. The reefing claw should be positioned roughly in the centre of the boom.

- Secure mainsheet — re-check.
- Shackle mainsail tack to the bow fitting, head to the jib halyard (make sure it is not twisted!).
- Larger boats often have hanks sewn into the jib luff which, starting at the tack, can be hanked onto the forestay.

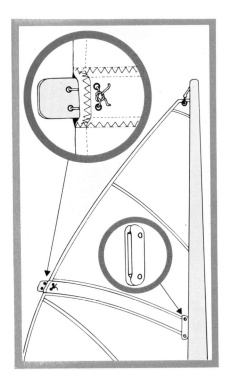

■ Secure jib sheet to clew (by means of shackles or knots) and finally, depending on the type of boat and size of jib, pass it through the jib sheet fairlead on the inside or outside of the shrouds (remember: figure of eight knots).

On some boats (e.g. Corsair, 470) the upper batten reaches from the leech to the mast. A plastic stopper is used to sit against the end of the batten which is tied to the leech (tension can be varied).

Typical mistakes made by beginners:
- *Jumping on board instead of stepping on carefully.*
- *Wearing dirty shoes.*
- *Leaving the sail or cockpit cover lying around on the quay.*
- *Everyone stepping on board on the same side and getting a ducking!*
- *Forgetting to lower the centreboard (for dinghies moored in the water).*
- *Not securing mainsail tack correctly.*
- *Not pulling mainsail foot far enough aft (creases).*
- *Shackling mainsail and jib to the halyards when they are twisted.*
- *Careless handling of halyard — halyard disappears upwards!*
- *Forgetting battens.*
- *Positioning the reefing claw too far aft on the boom (when the central pulley system is used).*
- *Forgetting figure of eight knots on the jib sheet ends.*
- *Mainsheet blocks twisted.*

Three ways of handling the mainsheet on small boats: 1 Simple centre pulley system with single block on the boom and double pulley block below. 2 Centre pulley system with traveller. 3 Stern pulley system.

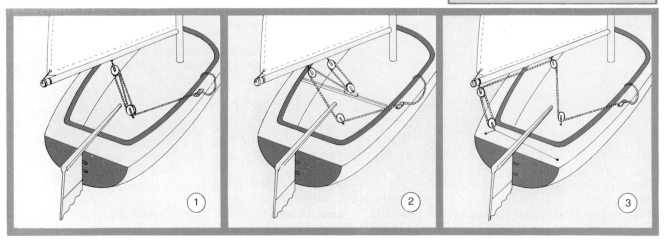

Hoisting Sail

It is usual to hoist sail from aft forwards, i.e. first the mainsail then the jib, to keep the boat lying well in the wind. However, this is not the case for a dinghy on land or a boat tied with fore and sternlines in a box. First of all pull the main halyard hand over hand, finally cleating it (if a cleat is available) and pulling with the other hand between cleat and mast head.

On many modern boats after the sail is hoisted the halyard is attached to a hook and tensioned by means of a tensioning lever. The sail may also be fixed to the mast head by means of a modern halyard lock.

The various ropes are then coiled up and tidied away (see p.32).

■ **Tip:**
To make hoisting the sail easier, the helmsman can lift up the boom from behind, being sure to release the kicking strap. In any case the main sheet should always be slack when hoisting or lowering sails.

Shouts of Command:
'Prepare to hoist the . . . sail!'
Reply: '... sail is ready to hoist!'
'Hoist the . . . sail!'

The jib is hoisted in the same way, after the appropriate commands. The job is much easier if you follow the example of the professionals and pull on the forestay which will then slacken and hang loose.

■ **Recommendation:** It is normal to cleat the mainsail halyard to starboard, and the jib halyard to port.

More Important Points:
In principle the mainsail is only hoisted when the boat is lying in the wind, when it is tied to a buoy or on the lee side of a jetty. (The jib can be hoisted as and when you wish.) If the boat is not in any of these positions you have three options open:
■ Move the boat round to the lee side.
■ Paddle to a buoy.
■ Paddle away from the jetty into the wind and then hoist sail.

If the conditions are right you could also sail away from the jetty with the jib only instead of paddling.

■ **Special tip:** Once you have paddled away from the jetty it is not so easy to stay in the wind while trying to hoist sail. The best thing to do is

On smaller boats hoisting the jib is very simple. Pull on the forestay like this with one hand and with the other pull the jib halyard which is looped over a cleat.

to paddle backwards till you have gathered a little speed and since the boat will point into the wind when making sternway you will gain enough time to hoist sail.

Typical mistakes made by beginners:
■ *The boat is not pointing into the wind when trying to hoist sail.*
■ *Mainsheet not slack enough. The wind fills the sail.*
■ *Mainsail badly set (folds on the luff).*
■ *Jib badly set (too much tension on the forestay and crooked edge to the wind).*

1

2

3

Taking in the Sails

As a rule take in the sails from fore to aft, i.e. start with the jib. There are, however, circumstances in which you would take in the mainsail first, e.g. if the jib is still in use. This would happen, for instance, if you were sailing into a harbour with the wind behind you, or when approaching a landing place from the windward side.

■ **Remember:** The boat must be pointing into the wind when you take the mainsail in.

Shouts of Command:
'Prepare to take in the . . . sail!'
('Prepare the main (or jib) halyard!')
Reply: ' . . . sail ready to take in!'
(or ' . . . halyard ready!')
'Take in . . . sail!'

When you take in the mainsail you must be careful not to drag the sail down but to pull on the luff where it joins the groove in the mast. The helmsman should grasp the boom, laying it carefully down — never dropping

Folding the mainsail on the boom:
1 Holding the leech and luff carefully fold up to boom.
2 Make a sort of pocket in the foot of the sail.
3 Secure the roll with the mainsheet. The sail head may either be unshackled or remain threaded in the mast groove. The neighbouring boat's sail leaves a lot to be desired!

1

2

3

4

it on the deck. A boom crutch can be used if available. Taking the boom down is made easier if the boat has a topping lift (yachts only — a line leading from the boom-end to the top of the mast).

Once the sails have been taken in, they should never be left lying around, even for a short time, since they could well catch the wind. The jib is either pulled from the bow towards the cockpit and secured on the mast, or completely removed. The mainsail is carefully folded on the boom and secured by means of the mainsheet or short ropes (see series of photographs). The elastic ties one often sees used for this purpose should not be used in our opinion since there is a danger of them striking the face and injuring the eyes if carelessly handled.

At the end of the day the sails are put away completely. The mainsail can be wrapped round the boom, but it is better if it is completely removed and laid out flat on dry ground. The battens

are then removed, and the sail is folded up like a fan (starting at the foot) and finally rolled up and placed in the bag (see series of photographs). The jib is either folded in the same way or better still, bearing in mind the metal luff, it should be rolled up into a loose tube-shape from tack to head and then folded and placed in the bag (see series of photographs).

When folding a mainsail it should first of all be laid flat on dry ground and the battens removed (1). It is then folded like a fan from the foot (2, 3), rolled up loosely, starting at the luff, and placed in the bag (4).

It is best to roll a jib in a tube shape (1) around its luff and then fold it up as shown (2).

1

2

Trimming and Setting the Sails

Setting the Sails

Setting the sails begins when a sail is hoisted — it must be pulled right to the top of the mast. The luff of the jib must be well tensioned to give a good entry to the wind, especially when sailing close-hauled. The foot and leech of the jib must be under the same tension when the jibsheet is pulled in; if they are not, the position of the **fairleads** should be adjusted if they are on a track.

- If the leech lifts, the fairlead should be moved forward.
- If the foot lifts, the fairlead should be moved aft.

If the fairleads are not adjustable the same effect can be achieved by heightening or lowering the jib tack.

Ideally, the mainsail should be set according to the wind conditions and course, i.e. the sail's curvature in profile is changed according to conditions.

- The stronger the wind, the flatter the sail. In light breezes the sail should have more fullness.
- On a close-hauled course a flatter sail is better; on a broad reach course or when sailing before the wind more fullness will result in greater forward propulsion.

If you do not have the equipment to alter the sail's fullness while sailing (as will be the case in small, simply equipped boats) you could before casting off:

Neither foot nor leech are lifting: fairlead correctly positioned.

The leech is lifting: move fairlead forward.

The foot is lifting: move fairlead aft.

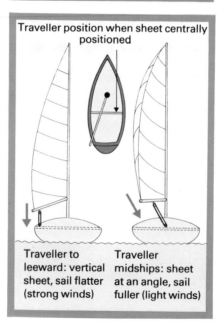

Traveller position when sheet centrally positioned

Traveller to leeward: vertical sheet, sail flatter (strong winds)

Traveller midships: sheet at an angle, sail fuller (light winds)

- Set the mainsail flat by tensioning the foot and luff, at the same time pulling the clew aft and securing it, and also pulling the boom down at the mast fitting (by means of the tack tensioner or lowering the carriage on the track).

Well-equipped boats (most racing boats) have the following equipment designed to alter the sail's profile: luff tensioner (cunningham system), foot tensioner, traveller and kicking strap.

The foot and luff are readily adjustable while sailing by means of the tensioning lines through the cunningham eyelet and over the tack, and the foot tensioning line on the boom.

The **traveller** consists of a track positioned across the cockpit (sometimes over the stern deck) in which a block for the mainsheet runs on a sliding carriage or a rope. Usually the carriage is moved by means of control lines which are belayed in jam cleats. You can adjust the sail curvature and the leech tension by moving the traveller to leeward or amidships as required.

- For a flatter sail profile (strong winds, gusts): sheet vertical on the boom: traveller moved outwards, i.e. to leeward.
- For a fuller sail profile (weaker winds): sheet slanting from the boom towards the midships axis (in extreme cases it may even be pulled to windward): traveller to windward (normally in the centre).

The simplest form of **kicking strap** is a small pulley system attached to the bottom of the mast which runs at an angle of approximately 45° to meet the boom about a quarter of the way along

In this picture of a Laser dinghy the kicking strap can be clearly seen attached to the boom.

its length. In this way, by pulling the boom downwards, you can alter the sail curvature and leech tension. It also prevents the boom from riding up on reaching and running courses.

Trimming the Sails

Use the main and jib sheets to trim the sails constantly so that you produce the best possible aerodynamic airflow round the sails. If your sails are correctly trimmed you can sail in the area of lift on all courses from hard on the wind to broad reach. As you get close to running before the wind, you will reach a point where the sails can no longer be kept in the area of lift and the favourable lee airflow begins to break away from the sail.

How do you trim your sails? As a rule of thumb remember:
- While sailing in the area of lift (close-hauled to broad reach) the sail should be eased just enough to prevent it from starting to lift.

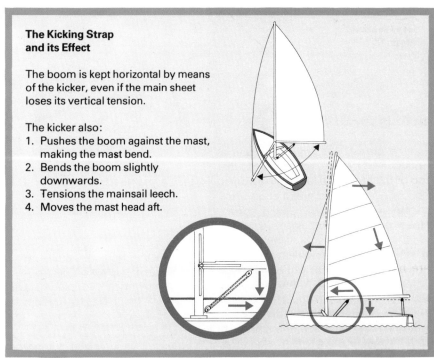

The Kicking Strap and its Effect

The boom is kept horizontal by means of the kicker, even if the main sheet loses its vertical tension.

The kicker also:
1. Pushes the boom against the mast, making the mast bend.
2. Bends the boom slightly downwards.
3. Tensions the mainsail leech.
4. Moves the mast head aft.

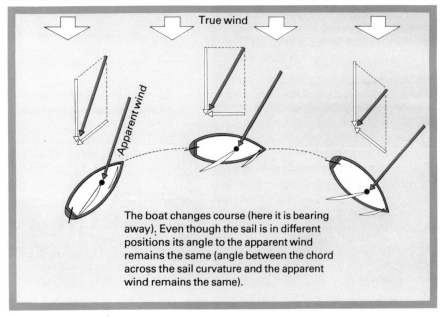

The boat changes course (here it is bearing away). Even though the sail is in different positions its angle to the apparent wind remains the same (angle between the chord across the sail curvature and the apparent wind remains the same).

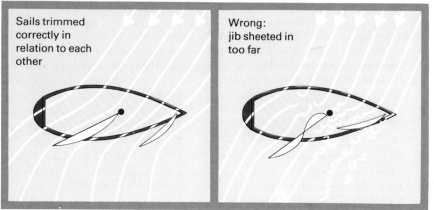

Sails trimmed correctly in relation to each other

Wrong: jib sheeted in too far

On dinghies and small keelboats the helmsman trims the mainsheet himself. On many yachts, however, the mainsheet is the crew's responsibility. Many sailing books state that the mainsheet must always be run through the hand on dinghies. This is only partially correct. Sheet cleats (e.g. jam cleats) are available, and are ideal devices for holding the sheets. If you have these on board, you should use them! In this way you can sheet the sails in so much better. And in an emergency it only requires one quick movement to free the sheets.

■ When sailing before the wind, ease the sheets as far as you can (do not let the boom hit the shroud).

It is important to keep a constant eye on the wind vane which will show you not only the wind direction (the apparent wind when sailing!) but also the changes in wind direction. Also use the wind vane to get the best trim for the sails. Rule of thumb:

■ When sailing in the area of lift trim the sails so that the headboard and wind vane remain parallel (wind vane blowing towards leech).

■ On a downwind course the wind vane will point exactly towards the bow.

On boats with a foresail it is important that both sails should be at approximately the same angle to the wind so that the airflow over the mainsail is not disrupted.

The sails can also be used to brake the boat. If you ease the sheets completely the sails begin to lift; they produce no more forward momentum and the boat slows down. Use the sheets to alter sail position constantly according to the wind. But remember:

■ Do not simply let the sheet rush out all at once: release it a little at a time, or you could find yourself too far to windward. On a dinghy you may even capsize to windward.

Typical mistakes made by beginners:
■ *Sails lifting unnecessarily.*
■ *Sails sheeted in too far.*
■ *Not watching wind vane.*
■ *Foresail sheeted in too far.*

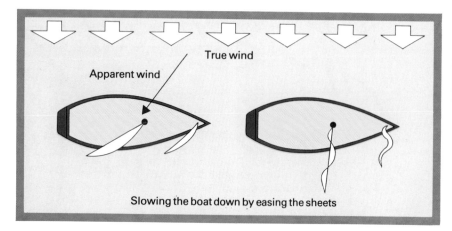

True wind

Apparent wind

Slowing the boat down by easing the sheets

Lateral and Longitudinal Trim — Steering

Sitting out and Trapeze

A sailing boat's trim is not only influenced by the different forces working on the sails. The position of the boat in the water must be constantly adjusted by the crew changing their position in the boat.

In medium to strong winds a boat will sail better if it is kept as upright as possible. The wind will catch the largest possible area of sail and produce the greatest forward momentum. You will also avoid the problem of carrying too much weather helm. In light breezes it is better to heel over slightly to lee, because in this position a better sail profile and therefore greater efficiency is achieved, and because the wetted area is less, so that there will be less friction. Heeling to windward is completely wrong (except in certain circumstances e.g. on a Finn or Optimist dinghy before the wind). Heeling — or the **lateral trim** — is controlled by correct positioning of the crew in the boat, or by *sitting out* if necessary. This is especially effective on dinghies, which rely to such a great extent on the influence of the crew's weight.

The helmsman should sit in the boat so that he holds the sheet with his right hand and the tiller, or tiller extension, with his left hand on a starboard tack. On a port tack it should be the other way round, i.e. he sits opposite the mainsail on the windward side. The

stronger the wind the further the crew has to sit out (on dinghies and small open keelboats the feet are pushed under the foot strap). The trapeze is used in extreme situations. If the wind is quite light, the helmsman should not sit on the side of the boat but on the floor. If the wind has dropped to such an extent that from this position there is no heeling leewards, then he should turn round and sit on the lee side. The same applies to the crew.

The fore-and-aft trim of the boat in the water — the **longitudinal trim** — is also very important if you want to achieve maximum speed.

If the stern is weighted down too much, eddies will form in the waterflow which will have a braking effect on the boat.

Therefore:
- The crew should move further forward, helmsman away from the tiller (use the tiller extension).
- If the wind is strong enough for planing on reaching courses the crew should move further aft.
- It may also be necessary to move aft on a course away from the wind if the bow is dipping down too far in the water.

A good crew will always be on the move, trying to improve the trim of the boat. This can be extremely exhausting, especially in squally weather.

Using the trapeze like this is very effective. The wire runs from the mast band and hooks onto the trapeze belt.

57

Typical sitting out position:
opposite the sail, feet high in the strap,
seat over the side, rounded back.
In spite of very strong winds this Laser is
being kept pretty well upright.

In very light breezes the boats should be
heeling to lee. We can clearly see here that
the helmsmen too are sitting on the lee
side.

Very bad position: too much weight aft,
the stern is too deep in the water and is
braking the boat. The helmsman's
position is appalling — he is getting in the
way of his own steering! The jib is sheeted
in too far in relation to the mainsail.

On a close-hauled course the entire crew
of this Soling is sitting out.

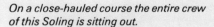

The 'pencil grip'.
Gripping the tiller extension from
underneath.

On a close-hauled course the helmsman is gripping the tiller extension from above, so his arm is in a very awkward position. The toe strap is too short, as well: the helmsman cannot get out far enough and the boat is heeling badly. Traveller further to lee would be better.

Here the extension is being gripped from above causing the wrist to bend awkwardly — it will soon start to ache! If this young crew had moved the traveller right over to lee, the sail on this close-hauled course would be flatter, making it easier to keep the boat upright.

Heeling too far: the toe strap is not being used. The helmsman is not sitting far enough out. Moving the traveller to lee would again help to stop the boat heeling so badly on this close-hauled course.

Tiller and Tiller Extension

So you can move about, using your weight to trim the boat, and so you can also slide towards the bow away from the stern and sit out if necessary on dinghies and dinghy-type keelboats, the tiller has to have an extended arm, a *tiller extension*. It would be impossible to sail a dinghy in strong winds without this piece of equipment.

■ If you want to develop a good steering technique, as used by racing sailors, then you must get used to using the 'pencil grip' right from the start.

Grip the tiller from below rather as you would hold a pencil (see photographs). This makes the arm position more natural and less cramped, especially when sitting out, and the arm muscles tire less easily. Very sensitive steering is possible in lighter breezes.

How to hold the tiller at a glance:
1 Normal sitting position (not sitting out), holding the extension just at the side of the body.
2 The extension could more easily be pushed down and damaged if gripped from above.
3 If you need to alter course so that the tiller has to be moved past the helmsman (usually when bearing away) it is best to pull the arm back and thus pull the tiller past the body. Do not . . .
4 . . . pull the extension on to the other side of the tiller and push away like this. It takes too long and you will lose your 'feeling' on the tiller.
5 You will also lose your sensitive 'touch' on the tiller if the extension is pulled across your stomach, forming a straight line with the tiller.
6 This position is to be avoided at all costs: the helmsman is sitting in the way of the tiller.

In harbour the rudder blade should always be fully raised.

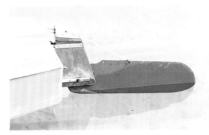
Impossible to sail with rudder blade not far enough down in the water.

Rudder blade still not far enough down in the water.

Correct position of rudder blade.

The Rudder

If you have a dinghy with a lifting rudder you must make sure that the rudder is positioned well down in the water till it is almost vertical (true for every course!). If the rudder blade is too horizontal in the water, the whole rudder will have to withstand very great pressures and may even break at the rudder head or tiller. Also if the boat is heeling badly there will not be enough of the blade in the water to have any effect at all!

As far as steering itself is concerned, you should remember one or two basic rules:

- Avoid violent movement of the rudder since it will brake the boat.
- Sensitive handling of the rudder means you will lose less speed.

- Moving the rudder further than you need will brake the boat.
- If necessary you can give the boat a little momentum by moving the rudder backwards and forwards. This is especially useful in very light winds or calm conditions. It is not allowed, however, during a race. Remember, though, that too violent a movement could damage the whole rudder apparatus.
- By carefully moving the tiller amidships and then pushing away hard, you can impart a turning moment to a motionless boat.

Do not be surprised if your sailing school does not immediately tell you to hoist sail and sail away but asks you to move your boat using a paddle. These exercises (one or two people paddling, one steering) are excellent for teaching beginners how to steer correctly (e.g. making circles, figures of eight, slaloming — forwards or backwards). Leave the sails in the boat house as they will only get in the way.

> **Typical mistakes made by beginners**
> - *Helmsman sits too far aft — longitudinal trim suffers. (Does not apply when planing.)*
> - *Too much rudder applied in strong winds.*
> - *In lighter breezes the boat is kept too upright or even made to heel to windward.*
> - *Helmsman not using tiller extension, although, because of the wind conditions, he should be sitting out and moving his weight forward.*
> - *Rudder blade not far enough down in the water.*
> - *Rudder moved too violently.*

Exercises with paddles are ideal to accustom the student to steering.
The paddle is held like this, looking in the direction you are going. It would have been better if the exercise could have been done without the sails on board.

Casting Off

Before Casting Off

If the boat is lying on the lee side of a jetty or a buoy, there is no problem: you can hoist sail straight away. Before casting off, however, it is a good idea to have a last look round the boat to make sure everything is in order. You can do without any nasty surprises once you are underway! The diagram may be helpful as a final check list.

Casting Off from a Jetty

■ If the boat is lying *alongside* the jetty with the wind more or less coming from the front on the *lee side* and you have room to get out to clear water, the crew simply pushes the bow out seawards from the jetty, sheeting the sails to the correct angle, and the manoeuvre is complete.

■ If the boat is lying alongside the jetty and there is no room aft, then put a fender over the stern, leave the aftspring tied till last, and after the crew has pushed the bow away, back the jib until the boat is far enough from the jetty.

■ If you are lying on the lee side and hemmed in on either side, or if the boat is tied with sternlines to posts, the boat will have to be taken out backwards (more information on making sternway is in the chapter *Sailing Astern*).

In this case we can use several methods for sailing astern:

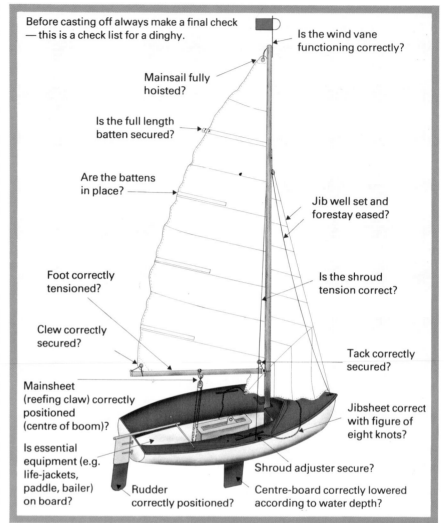

Before casting off always make a final check — this is a check list for a dinghy.

Is the wind vane functioning correctly?

Mainsail fully hoisted?

Is the full length batten secured?

Are the battens in place?

Jib well set and forestay eased?

Foot correctly tensioned?

Is the shroud tension correct?

Clew correctly secured?

Tack correctly secured?

Mainsheet (reefing claw) correctly positioned (centre of boom)?

Jibsheet correct with figure of eight knots?

Is essential equipment (e.g. life-jackets, paddle, bailer) on board?

Rudder correctly positioned?

Shroud adjuster secure?

Centre-board correctly lowered according to water depth?

1. The crew (or the person responsible for the forelines) pushes the boat away from the jetty. He should stand on the jetty with one foot on the front of the boat, balancing on the other leg. He must wait for the helmsman's command! Remember: push the boat out straight and try to avoid taking a flying leap on board!

2. The helmsman or a helper pulls the boat aft by the stern.

3. The helmsman backs the jib forward (also the mainsail) and sails out astern.

See the chapter *Hoisting Sail* for casting off from the windward side of a jetty.

Casting Off from a Buoy

Casting off from a buoy is basically easy. After hoisting the sails the buoy is simply thrown overboard on the windward side to prevent the boat sailing over the chain. If there is an on-shore wind you should not free the buoy until your boat has turned far enough away from the wind to let you sail away forwards immediately. Otherwise the boat could be driven backwards on to the shore, resulting in scratches at the very least.

Remember:
- Decide beforehand on which tack you are going to sail (there are often many boats about, and the wind direction makes one side better than the other).
- Turn out of the wind by backing the jib, or, often better, the mainsail.
- If the mainsail is backed the stern will usually turn away, e.g. mainsail backed to port — stern turns to star-

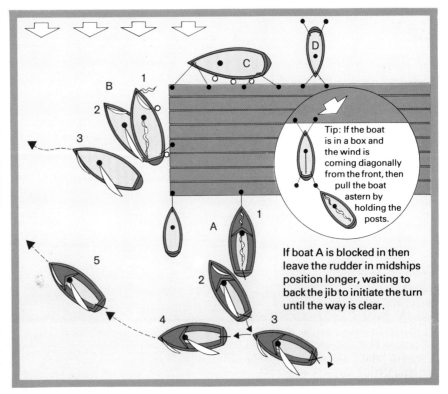

Tip: If the boat is in a box and the wind is coming diagonally from the front, then pull the boat astern by holding the posts.

If boat A is blocked in then leave the rudder in midships position longer, waiting to back the jib to initiate the turn until the way is clear.

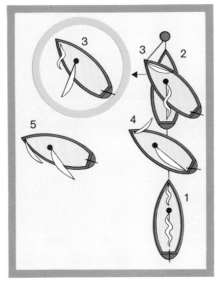

Casting off from a jetty: Boat A is lying on the lee side with its bow tied to the jetty. Boat B is lying alongside the jetty with the wind coming from the front. Boats C and D are lying on the windward side and may not therefore hoist sail. Boat A: after untying the foreline, jib is backed to starboard, rudder moved to starboard (sailing astern), and mainsail sheeted in tight (2). When boat has turned and has stopped (3), jib over, ease mainsail a little, now position rudder for forwards movement. Sheet in the sails for the course you are taking. Boat B: crew either simply pushes bow away or puts a fender over the stern, leaves the aftspring tied till last, backs jib to starboard, unties foreline (1), and sheets in mainsail.

Casting off from a buoy: 1 — hoist sail, then pull in on buoy (2). 3 — back jib (usually better to back mainsail), rudder positioned for sailing astern, untie; 4 — boat sails astern with jib back, sheet in mainsail.

board. (Remember: there are exceptions to this rule, e.g. with a Pirate!)
■ After you have untied from the buoy the boat will first of all make a little sternway. The rudder must be positioned initially for sailing astern.

Shouts of Command when Casting Off from a Buoy:
(First the commands for hoisting sail)
'Pull in to buoy to starboard/port!'
Reply: 'Buoy pulled in!'
'Clear the buoy!'
Reply: 'Buoy is clear!'
'Back the jib (mainsail) to starboard (port)!'
'Cast off forward!' Reply: 'Buoy away!'
'Jib over!' (or 'Mainsail over!')

Casting off from the lee side of a jetty. The boat has to sail astern a little way since there is a Laser next to it:
1 *Crew puts one foot on board and pushes boat back, tiller amidships.*
2 *Boat drifts astern — tiller still amidships.*
3 *Jib backed to port, rudder to port (tiller starboard).*
4 *Still drifting astern, rudder remaining to port, helmsman sheets in mainsail.*
5 *Since the boat is still moving, the rudder stays where it is; mainsheet eased a little.*
6 *Boat begins to move forward, jib over, rudder amidships. In order to pick up speed remember to avoid taking a close-hauled course straight away (sheet in mainsail accordingly).*

Typical mistakes made by beginners when casting off:
■ *Untying forelines too soon.*
■ *Boat makes a wrong turn when making sternway because rudder is turned the wrong way.*
■ *When sailing out of a gap, the boat is turned too early causing boat to collide with posts or neighbouring boats.*
■ *Forgetting to lower centreboard on a dinghy causing the boat to make leeway when curving round.*
■ *Sheeting in mainsail too late, therefore travelling too far astern.*
■ *Luffing up too far when beginning to sail forward, causing the boat to make leeway instead of picking up speed.*

Sailing Close-Hauled — Tacking

In the sailing theory section we have discussed how we can sail at a greater or lesser angle to the (true) wind up to about 45°. Sailing *close-hauled* and *hard on the wind* requires a great deal of experience and ability, and special emphasis is put on these courses during a race. Since the wind is coming diagonally from in front there is a strong tendency for a boat to *make leeway*; therefore on a dinghy never forget to keep the centre-board fully lowered. We have already discussed the crew's sitting position which is so important (see *Lateral and Longitudinal Trim — Steering*).

Finding the Sail Position

The sails are sheeted in tightly but not so tightly that the boat runs poorly. How, then, can the best possible sail position be found? Use the luff of the jib and mainsail to help you, ensuring that immediately the luff of the jib begins to lift you bear away till the lifting stops and then pull in the mainsail until it begins to lift, easing off a little till the lifting stops (see diagrams below). This is the correct sail position, and should not be altered; occasional wind irregularities should be corrected by means of steering.

> **Note:** Always watch the luffs and wind vane!

Making Use of Gusts

When sailing you constantly have to deal with gusts, both strong gusts (about which more later) and harmless gusts. Since a gust will change the apparent wind, you can quickly lose height when sailing close-hauled if you do not act quickly and turn it to your own advantage. How the apparent wind behaves and what you should do is shown in the diagrams on the next page.

Tacking

If you want to reach an objective lying directly to windward, then you have to *tack*, i.e. sail close-hauled on a zig-zag course to starboard and port alternately.

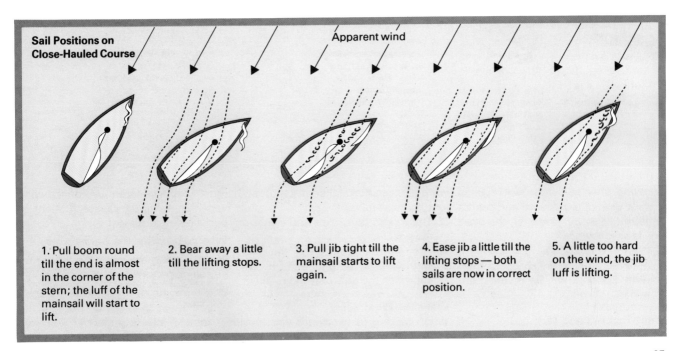

Sail Positions on Close-Hauled Course

Apparent wind

1. Pull boom round till the end is almost in the corner of the stern; the luff of the mainsail will start to lift.

2. Bear away a little till the lifting stops.

3. Pull jib tight till the mainsail starts to lift again.

4. Ease jib a little till the lifting stops — both sails are now in correct position.

5. A little too hard on the wind, the jib luff is lifting.

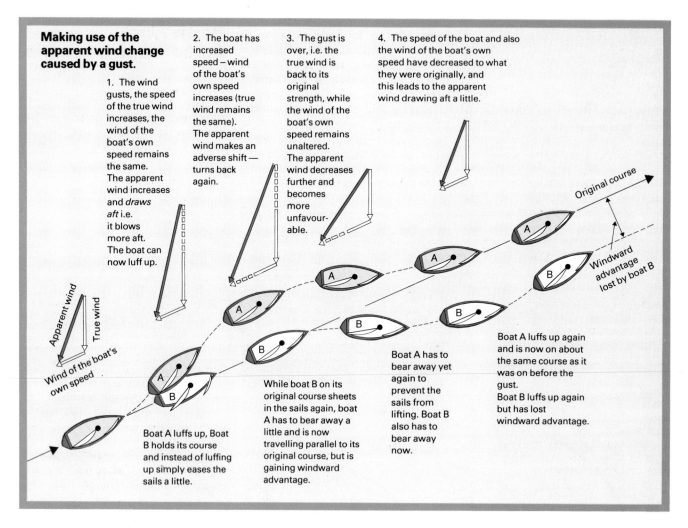

Making use of the apparent wind change caused by a gust.

1. The wind gusts, the speed of the true wind increases, the wind of the boat's own speed remains the same. The apparent wind increases and *draws aft* i.e. it blows more aft. The boat can now luff up.

2. The boat has increased speed – wind of the boat's own speed increases (true wind remains the same). The apparent wind makes an adverse shift — turns back again.

3. The gust is over, i.e. the true wind is back to its original strength, while the wind of the boat's own speed remains unaltered. The apparent wind decreases further and becomes more unfavourable.

4. The speed of the boat and also the wind of the boat's own speed have decreased to what they were originally, and this leads to the apparent wind drawing aft a little.

Apparent wind
True wind
Wind of the boat's own speed

Original course

Windward advantage lost by boat B

Boat A luffs up, Boat B holds its course and instead of luffing up simply eases the sails a little.

While boat B on its original course sheets in the sails again, boat A has to bear away a little and is now travelling parallel to its original course, but is gaining windward advantage.

Boat A has to bear away yet again to prevent the sails from lifting. Boat B also has to bear away now.

Boat A luffs up again and is now on about the same course as it was on before the gust.
Boat B luffs up again but has lost windward advantage.

Knowing when to change tack requires a great deal of experience and cannot be learnt in a day. However, the basic rule is as follows;

■ It is time to change tack when the goal lies abeam of your boat, otherwise the boat will be pointing unnecessarily high.

Short Tack — Long Tack

If the goal does not lie directly to windward you can make alternate short and long tacks as follows:

■ The longer tack takes you closer to the goal.

■ The shorter tack gives the boat windward advantage, and you will approach the goal only indirectly.

When the Wind Veers

When tacking to windward you must make use of the wind shifts, so you

must keep a constant eye on the wind vane for shifts (clockwise motion) or backs (anti-clockwise).

What to do when the wind veers:

■ If the wind draws aft (freer) luff up and gain more windward advantage.

■ If the wind draws forward (header) you must bear away. Note: if the wind shift lasts longer or if you have to bear away too far it would be

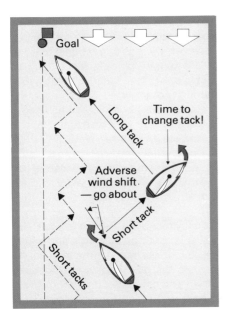

Goal

Time to change tack!

Long tack

Adverse wind shift — go about

Short tack

Short tacks

better to go about and make use of the shift on the other tack.

Long or Short Tacks?
Theoretically long tacks are better since you lose the least amount of speed because you have to turn less.

Corsairs tacking in a race. You can see the direction of the true wind by looking at the yacht moored to the buoy.

Unfortunately the wind is never constant enough for long tacks to be practical. If the wind shifts adversely at the end of a long tack, you have lost time by pointing the boat unnecessarily high. If, on the other hand, the shift is favourable after going about you would be sailing on the unfavourable tack. Therefore, as a rule it is better not to stray too far from the line joining your starting point and your objective, i.e. make the tacks shorter.

Typical mistakes made by beginners:
- *Mainsail sheeted in too far.*
- *Jib sheeted in too far.*
- *Jib lifting.*
- *Not making use of gusts, headers and freers.*
- *Bearing away too far in headers instead of going about.*
- *Sailing too long on the short tack, pointing boat unnecessarily high.*

Beam Wind — Broad Reach — Planing

If you travel far enough to leeward that you are no longer sailing close-hauled, you will find yourself on a *reaching course*.
Remember:
- If the true wind is blowing exactly from the side then it is a beam wind (a reaching course).
- If the true wind is blowing more astern than from the side, you will be on a broad reaching course.

Note: The faster the boat's speed the more the apparent wind will blow from the front.

On a reaching course the boat will attain its highest speeds and the conditions will be quieter. The sail position is adjusted according to the course since the goal can be approached direct.

Since the boat will make less leeway the more you bear away from a close-hauled to a reaching course, the centre-board on a dinghy may be raised halfway (at high speeds or in winds more aft than beam). Advantage: the wetted area becomes smaller and the boat travels faster; it will also rectify the boat's tendency to carry weather helm on these courses. Since on reaches the sail has to be eased, the mainsheet pulls diagonally on the boom, giving the boom a tendency to ride up.

- The *kicking strap* (if available) must be used to stop the boom from riding

This Corsair is planing in a very well-balanced position on a course between a reach and a broad reach. Because of the high speed the apparent wind is blowing more from the front than from the side, therefore the sails are sheeted in further than usual.

Planing on a broad reach in wind force 7. You can see the stern wave being left behind. The upright trim of the boat is excellent here — only an expert is able to do this in such a strong wind.

up. If the sails are not too slack, move the traveller leeward to allow the sheet a more vertical pull (see also chapter Trimming and Setting the Sails).

It is important to make use of the gusts or the boat will luff up by itself:

■ Bear away in gusts and ease the sheets — never luff up.

Spinnakers can be used on reaches and the boat can be made to **plane** (see also chapter Planing). If the wind is very strong, heavily-built dinghies and light keelboats such as the Y.W. Dayboat or Tempest can be made to plane. Modern light dinghies, e.g. the Finn, F.D. and 470, will plane at about wind force 3–4.

Planing in a light dinghy is one of the most fascinating aspects of sailing. However, there is a great deal to do to keep a dinghy planing for as long as possible. A few aids to help your **planing technique**:

■ Raise centre-board about half way.
■ Crew further aft than usual.
■ Adjust kicking strap firmly.
■ Do not allow the boat to run too hard into the waves, but if possible sail around and over the waves.
■ Keep the boat upright.

It is easy to initiate planing in a gust, for example: bear away a little and adjust the sails (usually ease the sheets). As soon as the gust begins to die down, luff up and carefully tighten the sheets to help you plane for as long as possible. To plane for longer periods you should keep adjusting the sheets. In a good long planing wind, the sheets must be pulled tighter after the initial increase in speed since the apparent wind shifts adversely due to the higher speed.

Typical mistakes made by beginners
■ *Sheets not eased enough.*
■ *Jib sheeted in too far compared with mainsail.*
■ *Kicking strap not adjusted firmly.*
■ *Boat allowed to luff up in gusts.*

Running Before the Wind

The wind is blowing directly from behind, the sails are eased off as far as possible to starboard or port. The jib is now taken in and a spinnaker hoisted. Or the jib can be *boomed out* (held out on the opposite side to the mainsail). In light breezes running before the wind is very pleasant and harmless, the boat runs nicely and does not heel.

Remember:

- Raise the centre-board, perhaps leaving a tiny section lowered to counteract any possible yawing.
- No matter how tempted you are to raise the rudder it should be left completely lowered (see *The Rudder*).
- In gusts you should give counter-rudder to prevent the boat from going off course (luffing up).

In strong winds running before the wind has its pitfalls:

- It is easy to underestimate the strength of the true wind since the apparent wind is weaker.
- The stronger the wind and the higher the waves are running the more off course the boat is thrown, i.e. it *yaws*. The helmsman has to be on his toes to keep correcting with the rudder.
- The boat begins to shake unpleasantly along its long axis.
- There is the danger of the boom swinging suddenly round to the other side. This is called an *involuntary gybe* and it can damage the gear, cause a dinghy to capsize and

even result in a fatal accident (if the boom hits someone on the head).

The pitfalls can be avoided if in strong winds and high waves you avoid sailing before the wind altogether by tacking towards your goal using broad reach tacks. On larger boats (ocean-going yachts) there is usually a *boom preventer*, a rope leading from the end of the main boom to the bow to hold it firm.

Typical mistakes made by beginners

- *Sail not eased off enough.*
- *Jib sheeted in too far instead of being boomed out on the other side.*
- *Luffing up in a gust.*
- *Forgetting to raise centre-board.*

1

2

3

1 On a downwind course the mainsail is eased right off. In strong winds this course is very difficult to sail and is often avoided even by expert sailors.

2 While the boat in the foreground is sailing before the wind (the helmsman is trying to counteract yawing) the other two boats have luffed up a little and are sailing more on a broad reach.

3 The spinnaker is a typical sight on many classes of boat when running before the wind (also on broad reach courses).

Going About

Going about is the 'classical' manoeuvre when tacking, e.g., if you are sailing close-hauled on a *starboard tack* the boat is made to go about by turning its bow through the wind, and it can then sail to the *port tack*.

> **Important:** To go about the boat must first of all be on a close-hauled course. On a reach course, for example, you would first of all have to luff up and sheet in the sails or you would lose so much speed that the sails would start to lift and you would come to a standstill!

Before this manoeuvre the helmsman should give the command 'Ready about!'. The crew clears the jibsheet and replies 'All clear!'. The helmsman now gives the order 'Lee-Ho!', moves the rudder to leeward and the bow goes to windward and turns through the eye of the wind until he can set the rudder for the new course. Meanwhile the crew eases the jib so that he can set it again on the other side. Immediately the jib is backwinded it is moved over. If the jib is large this must be done at precisely the right moment so that it does not catch the wind.

The mainsail remains sheeted in and can be left cleated. Racing sailors often ease the mainsheet a little so that they can pick up speed quickly on the new tack, not too close to the wind.

Special going about technique: for boats such as Pirate, Corsair, 470, 420, F.D., Tempest etc. If they have a tiller extension the following procedure is recommended.

1 Close-hauled course, e.g. here on starboard tack ('Ready about!')

2 Boat heads into the wind ('Lee-Ho!'), helmsman has already moved his right foot to the new side.

3 Boat turns through the wind, crew ducks under boom.

7 Finally the sitting positions are taken up again.

6 The right hand now takes hold of the mainsheet.

The observant reader will have noticed that the rudder is not correctly lowered. Explanation: the water was too shallow during this demonstration.

If the turn is incorrectly carried out, e.g. if you do not have enough speed, you may find it difficult to turn through the wind. This is often the case with heavy yachts when the waves are running high, and also with catamarans. In these circumstances the jib is left aback to help the boat about. Final command: 'Jib over!'.

5 The body has to be turned round while standing (both sails are pulling), the previous sheet hand (left) now grasps the extension behind the back.

The **shouts of command** once again:
'Ready about!' Reply: 'All clear!'
'Lee-Ho!' 'Jib over!'

Some Points of Detail and Tips
- Do not move the rudder too violently. You will turn quickly but lose speed.
- Only go about if the boat has enough momentum.
- Do not turn into large waves.
- Keep the sails pulling for as long as possible and do not allow to lift.
- Change places in good time so that you can trim immediately.
- A good moment to go about is when the boat is headed by an adverse wind shift and the new tack becomes

4 When it is time to ease the jib (3 is already a little too late!), the helmsman stands up holding the tiller extension vertical.

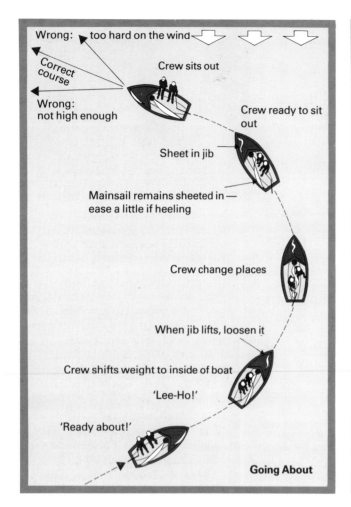

Wrong: too hard on the wind

Correct course

Wrong: not high enough

Crew sits out

Crew ready to sit out

Sheet in jib

Mainsail remains sheeted in — ease a little if heeling

Crew change places

When jib lifts, loosen it

Crew shifts weight to inside of boat

'Lee-Ho!'

'Ready about!'

Going About

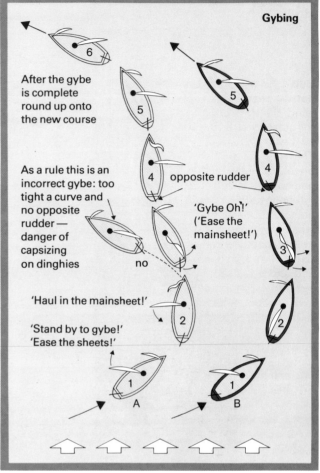

Gybing

After the gybe is complete round up onto the new course

As a rule this is an incorrect gybe: too tight a curve and no opposite rudder — danger of capsizing on dinghies

opposite rudder

'Gybe Oh!' ('Ease the mainsheet!')

no

'Haul in the mainsheet!'

'Stand by to gybe!' 'Ease the sheets!'

A

B

more advantageous.

- A boat is headed when it heels further to leeward. The following trick is then possible: just before going about the crew moves further into the boat from the sitting out position, thus allowing the boat to heel. Without rudder pressure the boat will now turn into the wind. The rudder is positioned and the turn completed.

Typical mistakes made by beginners:

- *Rudder moved too fast — brakes boat.*
- *Going about from a reach course without first sheeting in the sails and luffing up: loss of speed.*
- *Not bearing away enough after going about, sails lifting.*

- *After going about the boat bears away too far: height is lost as well as speed because of the incorrect sail position.*
- *Trying to go about with not enough momentum, the boat 'dies'.*
- *Easing jib too soon; it will then lift without pulling.*

Gybing

Gybing is also a way of changing tacks, not by turning the bow through the wind, but by bearing away and turning the stern through the wind.

The mainsail, which has been completely eased when before the wind, is hauled over to the other side, and then the boat luffs up again. In contrast to going about the loss of speed is very small, if there is any loss of speed at all. The manoeuvre can therefore be carried out at full speed. In strong winds and under full sail the gybe should be executed with extreme care. It can be avoided altogether by using the *tacking round* method (see following pages).

If, without changing course, you sail before the wind and you simply haul the mainsail over to the other side, e.g. because of a wind shift, or for tactical reasons to do with right of way in a race, then this procedure is called **gybing on the run**.

Gybing (p.72): If the wind is strong in phase 2 there is danger of an involuntary gybe for boat A. Boat B avoids this danger by sheeting in the mainsail before it has finished bearing away (2). Then, with tight mainsail, the stern turns through the wind (3). Mainsail is immediately eased off and opposite rudder given (not too much!).

Procedure

From a broad reach, bear away a little to a run, at the same time easing the sails. The mainsail should be sheeted in as far as possible. The sail should now move over amidships ('Gybe Oh!'). This is achieved by a careful and gentle 'oversteering', i.e. bearing away from the before the wind course.

It is now vital to remember two things that will prevent the boat gaining a very strong turning moment towards the new luff side with violent heeling, and danger of capsizing:
1. Ease the mainsail immediately on the new side.
2. Counteract the tendency to turn to the new windward side, i.e. turn again till just before the wind, by giving *opposite* or *counter-rudder*.

As soon as this is done and the mainsail is eased and counter-rudder given, you can alter course to the new windward heading, and the manoeuvre is complete.

> **Shouts of Command**:
> 'Stand by to gybe!' Reply: 'All clear!'
> 'Ease the sheets!'
> 'Haul in the mainsheet!'
> 'Gybe Oh!'
> 'Ease the mainsheet!'
> 'New course: Haul in . . .!'

These shouts of command are essential on yachts if the helmsman is not responsible for the mainsheet himself. On boats where the helmsman is responsible for the sheet, a shortened version of these commands is usually enough:

'Stand by to gybe!'... 'All clear!' 'Gybe Oh!'

Further observations

Before beginning to gybe, if you bear away so that you are exactly before the wind, there is the danger of an involuntary gybe if the wind is strong and the waves running high, since it is more difficult to control a rolling boat. In such cases it is better to sheet in the mainsail before reaching a before the wind course (on a broad reach) and only then bear away and turn through the wind. It is worth considering whether it would be safer to do it this way, especially on yachts, since any initial tendency to heel does not matter.

Technique

Normally the mainsail is sheeted in and eased by means of the mainsheet running through blocks. On boats where the helmsman is responsible for both tiller and sheet he must theoretically use both hands for the mainsheet and keep hold of the tiller at the same time! There is only one technique possible and this is recognised internationally:
■ As soon as the boat approaches the run (as soon as the crew has moved its weight towards the inside of the boat) the helmsman stands up, jams the tiller between his knees and steers by moving his knees right and left (see photographs p.74 left).

The legs are used in this way by racing sailors throughout the world when hoisting, taking in and moving over the spinnaker, whenever the helmsman needs both hands for the spinnaker halyard.

4

3

2

1

The racing sailor uses a slightly different gybe technique on dinghies and smaller keelboats which we call a **slam gybe**. Instead of pulling the sheet through the blocks he grasps the entire tackle and 'throws' the boom over in one movement (see series of photographs right).

Practise this variation only in extremely light winds which are not strong enough to push out the mainsail when eased. This is an ideal practice situation for beginners.

It should also be mentioned that a fast gybe carried out from a close-hauled course is the best evasive action to take when going about is impossible. You bear away very quickly without having enough time to ease the sheets properly (sheet eased all at once), the mainsail is then moved over and opposite rudder given (as usual), and finally you bear away as required.

3

2

1

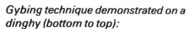

Gybing technique demonstrated on a dinghy (bottom to top):
1 Boat almost before the wind, the crew has moved its weight to the inside of the boat. Helmsman takes up his position: tiller between knees, both hands holding the sheet.
2 Mainsail sheeted in tight.
3 'Oversteering', i.e. in this case the helmsman pushes his knees to starboard, till the mainsail tries to go over to the other side.
4 As soon as the mainsail goes over it is eased, and the helmsman simultaneously pushes his knees to port to give the necessary opposite rudder. Now they can luff up again and the crew will sit on the port side.

'All standing gybe' (from bottom to top):
As soon as the boat is running the helmsman takes up his initial position: legs apart, he takes hold of the sheet with the near hand (here, the left hand on a port tack) (1). With one movement he pulls the boom over to the other side (2 & 3), giving more or less opposite rudder depending on the strength of the wind.

Tips

- Do not gybe in a gust. When the weather is bad carry out your gybe (if you absolutely have to) when the pressure of the apparent wind is at its smallest, i.e. when the boat is at its highest speed in relation to the wind.
- On dinghies the centre-board should be pulled up three-quarters of the way, or even completely. As a result the boat will slip to leeward in strong winds, thus lessening the degree of heel. Therefore: when the centre-board is raised the danger of cap-sizing is reduced!
- If you find giving opposite rudder difficult, simply forget what you are trying to do and aim to steer on a run again. You should then find the problem is solved.

Typical mistakes made by beginners:

- *Sail does not go over because you fail to 'oversteer' when sailing before the wind with sails sheeted in tight.*
- *No opposite rudder after 'Gybe Oh!' — tendency to heel in strong winds.*
- *Too much opposite rudder, and boom swings back.*
- *After 'Gybe Oh!' the sail is eased too slowly and not enough — tendency to heel.*
- *Centre-board left lowered on dinghies, leading to danger of capsizing.*

Tacking Round Method

This simply means that you go about instead of making a gybe. The manoeuvre is used in very strong winds when you do not want to attempt a gybe and you can go about instead. From a reach, instead of bearing away you luff up, go about and then bear away again.

Important:

- Luff up only to a close-hauled course making sure the sails are correctly sheeted in.

If the sails are not correctly sheeted in or you attempt to go about direct from a reach course, you will lose so much momentum that the whole manoeuvre will fail.

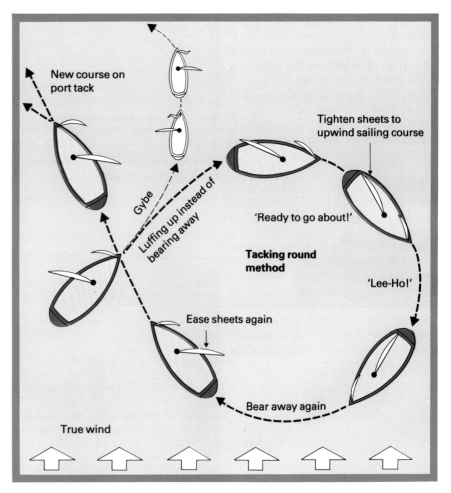

New course on port tack

Gybe

Luffing up instead of bearing away

Tighten sheets to upwind sailing course

'Ready to go about!'

Tacking round method

'Lee-Ho!'

Ease sheets again

Bear away again

True wind

Heaving To

If you want to bring your boat almost to a standstill and hold it on one spot across the course of the waves, you should use the 'heaving to' manoeuvre. The jib is held aback into the wind, and the mainsail is slackened off. The tiller is pushed to the leeward side, i.e. on the opposite side to the jib. The rudder remains in this position. To avoid the mainsail lifting too much you can sheet it in slightly. Every boat will react a little differently to heaving to, but in general heeling will be minimised to a great extent because this is a stable position to the wind. The boat, which is lying almost across the course of the waves, will be thrust very slightly forwards and very slowly leewards.

'Heaving to' is also used by ocean-going yachts to weather a storm. In this case the reefed mainsail, or, better still, trysail, is sheeted in. Heaving to is a universal manoeuvre and is taught by some sailing schools very early in the curriculum. It is useful if you need to do some repairs, or if you need to reef, and it enables you to go alongside other boats so that you can get near the starting line in a race. It is also used when pulling someone who has fallen into the water back on board.

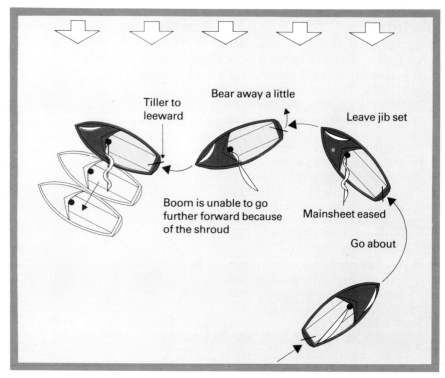

Tiller to leeward

Bear away a little

Leave jib set

Boom is unable to go further forward because of the shroud

Mainsheet eased

Go about

Heaving to is best done by easing the sheets on a reach course and letting the boat drift round. Then the jib is held back and the rudder set to windward. A boat can be very quickly hove to in this way after going about.

A hove to 470 dinghy. Clearly visible are the backed jib, the eased mainsail and the tiller pushed to leeward.

Sailing Astern

There are very many circumstances when you need to sail astern.
For example:
- When casting off from the lee side of a jetty.
- When casting off from a buoy.
- When hoisting sail on the water.
- When your boat 'dies' when going about in strong winds.
- When you tack in a narrow harbour, or because of some obstacle you need to go back a little.
- When, before the start of a race, you need to manoeuvre into a gap or want to get out of a situation where you are hemmed in.

Although it is more or less a question of 'drifting' backwards rather than actually sailing it is a good idea to practise sailing astern on smaller boats until you are fully confident of the manoeuvre.

Sailing astern is possible by:
- Letting yourself drift through the wind.
- The crew gripping the jib at the clew and holding it as far out as possible.
- Backing the mainsail.

The best method to practise is that using the backed mainsail. The rudder position is vital when sailing astern; it should be kept almost amidships and moved very little.

> **Note**: The stern will turn in the direction in which the rudder blade is pointing.

Tips for Practice

- In a slight breeze and with plenty of room go head to wind and wait till the boat is standing still. Then push the main boom forward and hold the rudder amidships.
- If the boat tries to turn towards the backed sail, push the tiller towards the sail (or parallel to the wind vane), until you are sailing directly downwind.
- For your first attempts you could go head to wind towards a jetty, the crew simply pushing you back.
- If you are travelling too fast simply let the sail out a little.

Going Head to Wind

In the chapter *Trimming and Setting the Sails* it was said that by freeing the sheets, e.g. on a reach course, you can slow the boat down. This 'braking' effect can be increased by steering the boat directly into the wind.

> **Note:** Head to wind means the true wind — you must therefore find out where it is coming from by looking at the wave formations, boats at anchor or moored to buoys, flags, smoke etc.

Sailing head to wind is the 'classic' method of approaching a windward goal (buoy or jetty) from the lee side and stopping so that the boat can be tied up.

Although it is possible to sail head to wind from every course, it is best to sail towards an imaginary point from which you are going to start the manoeuvre on a *reaching course*. By doing this you have the best possible opportunity of correcting your course since it is easy both to bear away and luff up.

The main difficulty is to estimate the required distance for your *run up* and this is dependent on boat weight, wind and waves, and also the speed of the boat as it turns into the wind.
Basic things to remember:
- A heavy boat carries its weight further than a lighter boat.
- A very light boat (planing dinghy) will come to a standstill far quicker

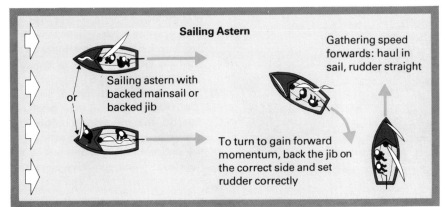

Sailing Astern

Sailing astern with backed mainsail or backed jib

or

Gathering speed forwards: haul in sail, rudder straight

To turn to gain forward momentum, back the jib on the correct side and set rudder correctly

Lifting up the main boom on boats with no kicking strap — ideal to free the mainsheet.

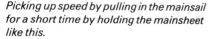

Picking up speed by pulling in the mainsail for a short time by holding the mainsheet like this.

Braking trick when going head to wind — backing the mainsail; should be practised by the helmsman on smaller boats.

than a heavy boat, so it only needs a short run up.

- The stronger the wind and the higher the waves are running the faster all boats will stop.
- When going head to wind, the faster the rudder is moved the greater its braking effect i.e. the run up distance is smaller.

Shouts of Command:
'Ready to go head to wind!'
Reply: 'All clear!'
'Free the sheets' (or if the jib has been taken in: 'Free the main sheet!')

Tips

- If, after you have gone head to wind, you find you are travelling too fast towards your goal, you can brake small boats very elegantly by backing the mainsail (for a short time only, or if necessary, several short movements).
- If you think you have overestimated the run-up distance required, you can carefully luff up and free the sheets at a later stage; the boat will then lose less speed.
- Make sure the mainsheet is completely free. You can test this by grasping the boom quickly and lifting it up for a short time (only boats with no kicking strap!), or press it out to the side.
- If you think your dinghy is going to 'die' before reaching your goal you can do the following: before the boat stops, bear away a little, hold the entire mainsheet and pull in the mainsail. When you have picked up enough speed, turn towards your goal again.

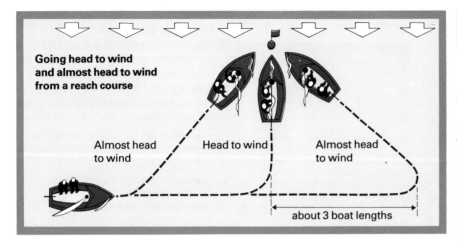

Going head to wind
and almost head to wind
from a reach course

Almost head
to wind

Head to wind

Almost head
to wind

about 3 boat lengths

Almost Head to Wind

This is a variation of the (direct) head to wind manoeuvre, used especially in the man overboard drill. The boat does not turn directly against the wind, but at a slight angle to it (close-hauled, but with free sheets). The starting-off point is about three boat lengths in front of or behind the point where you would turn to go directly head to wind. It is useful because if the boat is in danger of stopping too soon you can pick up speed a little by pulling in the mainsheet (before it comes to a complete standstill!).

Note: It is important when going almost head to wind that the mainsheet is completely free, so that the boom can swing out far enough to the side (push the boom away for a short time).

It is easier to start an almost head to wind manoeuvre from behind the point for the direct head to wind turn, since it

is easier for the inexperienced sailor to judge the various distances from this point. However, the boat has to turn through the wind and in extreme conditions this can cause problems.

Typical mistakes made by beginners:

■ *You do not find out where the true wind is coming from and therefore you will find you are not directly head to wind.*

■ *Mainsheet not freed, so if the wind veers the mainsail could catch the wind and the boat will pick up speed.*

■ *Boat approaching goal too fast means you did not turn at the correct time.*

■ *The boom has been backed for too long and your boat 'dies' before reaching your goal!*

■ *When turning almost head to wind, the boat does not slow down enough because main sheet is not freed.*

Preparation

Once you have mastered the head to wind manoeuvre mooring should pose no problems. Before you carry out the manoeuvre, however, you should make sure you have all the information you need: e.g. position of jetty or harbour entrance, wind direction, water depth, position of boats at anchor which could get in the way. Then prepare the mooring lines, fenders, and boathook, and, on a dinghy raise the centre-board a little (only if the water is shallow). And, of course, think through how you are going to carry out the manoeuvre.

Jetty, Lee Side

The main element in approaching the lee side of a jetty is going head to wind, which you should do, if possible, on a beam reach. The manoeuvre described in most books involves taking in the jib before going head to wind. By doing this you will avoid unnecessary lifting which could damage the cloth, and prevent the jib from swinging aback involuntarily; also, the man responsible for the forelines has more room at the bow. In practice, however, especially on dinghies, most good sailors leave the jib set so that if the turn into the wind misfires, they can sail away from the jetty more easily by holding the jib aback.

Normally you should tie up a boat bow to jetty, ideally in such a way that the

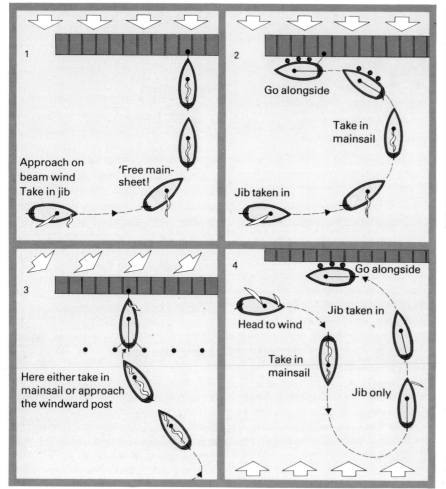

Shouts of Command:

'Ready to approach jetty (on port/
starboard!'
(and if the jib has to be taken in, the
appropriate commands)
'Ready to head into wind!'
Reply: 'All clear!'
'Free sheets!' ('Free mainsheet!')
'Clear the forelines (sternlines/
fore/aftsprings)!'
Reply: 'Forelines (etc) clear?'
'Forelines/sternlines on land!'
'Tie forelines (sternlines . . .)!'
'Forelines (sternlines) tied!'

Buoy

Coming into a buoy on the lee side
involves exactly the same procedure as
approaching a jetty. It is, however,
somewhat easier since you cannot
bump the boat if you are travelling too
fast. Never grasp the buoy when sailing
past if you have started the turn in too
late as this will result in an unpleasant
pirouette! You must start again from
the beginning. On a yacht with high
topsides don't forget to have a boathook handy or the crew will have to
perform some interesting acrobatics
when trying to grasp the buoy.

Shouts of Command:

'Ready to approach buoy!'
'Ready to take in jib!'
(or 'Prepare jib halyard!')
Reply: 'Jib ready to take in!'
(or 'Jib halyard ready!')
'Take in jib!'
'Ready to head into wind!'
Reply: 'All clear!'
'Free mainsheet!'
Reply: 'Buoy clear!'

crew can step off with the foreline
without have to brake the boat at all.

On a larger yacht, however, it is safer to
go alongside if there is room after
having taken in the mainsail while head
to wind. It is not a good idea, in fact it
could be dangerous, to try to stop a
heavy yacht by pushing it back.

*1 Approaching the lee side of a jetty head
to wind.*
*2 With a larger yacht it is best to go
alongside on the lee side.*
*3 If the wind is blowing diagonally, it is
possible to enter a box on the lee side in
this way.*
*4 Approaching the windward side of a
jetty.*

Jetty, Windward Side

The lee side of a jetty is often full and it is therefore important to be able to approach a jetty on the windward side, i.e. the side the wind is blowing towards.

Procedure
- On a beam wind and with main halyard prepared sail in front of your mooring spot (a few boat lengths away) and then turn head to wind (away from mooring!).
- As soon as the boat is lying head to wind, take in the mainsail.
- When the mainsail is taken in make use of the remaining speed and steer the boat round 180° (if necessary back the jib to aid turning).
- With eased jib run before the wind. Steer towards jetty; prepare the jib halyard in plenty of time.
- Before you reach your mooring take in the jib (the stronger the wind the earlier you should do this).
- If there are no posts for the lines, then go alongside the jetty (unless you are going to use a stern anchor) and put out the fenders. Note: if on a large, heavy dinghy you raise the centre-board before going alongside, the resultant heeling will take you nicely to the jetty.

Note: If there are no posts for the stern lines or if you do not have a good stern anchor you should never leave a boat on the windward side unattended.

Shouts of Command:
(First of all prepare the main halyard)
'Ready to head into wind!'
'All clear!'
'Free sheets'/'Take down mainsail!'
(If necessary: 'Back jib to starboard/port'/'Jib over!')
(Commands to take in jib)
'Clear the forelines (sternlines/fore- and aftsprings)!'
'All clear!'
'Take …lines (…springs) on land!' '…on land!'
If required: 'Stop boat slowly!'
(If necessary: commands to bring out more lines)

Typical mistakes made by beginners
- *Main halyard prepared too late; impossible, therefore, to take in mainsail quickly enough when head to wind (boat turns away again…).*
- *Forget to take in the jib, boat travels too fast towards jetty.*
- *Boat not taken alongside jetty, so absence of posts for sternlines will cause problems!*

Approaching the lee side of a jetty on a dinghy. On small boats such as this it is not absolutely necessary to take in the jib beforehand. The boat (here a Pirate) makes its approach on a beam wind (1), then the sheets are freed and the boat turns against the wind (2). While the boat drifts towards the jetty, the forelines are prepared (3 & 4). The crew is standing on the foredeck holding the forelines (obscured by the jib). She grasps a post on the jetty (5) and steps off with the foreline (6)

Man Overboard Drill

Although a man overboard is not an everyday occurrence because of the many safety devices found on board today (guard rail on cruising yachts, safety harness and safety lines) it is nevertheless essential that every responsible sailor knows the drill and is able to carry it out if necessary. To practise the procedure use a buoy, or a container filled with water or similar, to replace the 'man'.

If someone falls overboard, then immediately after the shout 'man over board!', throw a lifebelt over and designate one crew member to maintain a constant watch on the person in the water. These points are very important when sailing on coastal waters or on the high seas; less so for inland waters and smaller boats. If you are sailing a 470 it is unlikely you will have a lifebelt on board, and if the crew falls over board, there is no one left to keep an eye on him!

There are three possible courses of action:
1. Drill using a gybe and then going almost head to wind.
2. Drill using the going about method and then going almost head to wind.
3. Drifting and heaving to.

There are many different opinions as to the advantages and disadvantages of these methods, and it is therefore best left to the individual sailing schools to decide which one they recommend.

Drill using a Gybe or Going About

If you are on a close-hauled course, it is best to use the gybing method (if you have rejected the drift method) — so long as you are confident that the wind strength is suitable.

- Sail on about three boat lengths to gain windward advantage, then turn leeward, gybe and luff up so that you can approach the practice buoy on a beam wind.

If you are unsure about gybing from a close-hauled course, or if the boat is on a beam reach or before the wind, then you can consider using the going about method.

- From a close-hauled course immediately bear away on to a reach (from a broad reach course you sail a little further, and from a run you luff up), luff up into the wind, go about, bear away again on a reach course and approach the buoy almost head to wind.

> **Shouts of Command:**
> After the initial cry of 'Man over board!' the commands for going about or gybing are used depending on which method is being employed.

Head to Wind
The approach to the person in the water should never be directly head to wind since there is a danger of the bow hitting them. An indirect approach should always be used as this will take you alongside the person, and you can also influence the 'run up' by adjusting the mainsheet.

As has already been discussed in the chapter *Head to Wind* it is possible to approach a goal indirectly by making your turning point either before or after the point at which you would turn directly into the wind.

There are differing opinions as to which is best, and we do not wish to recommend one rather than the other. However, the following facts should be borne in mind:
1. The indirect approach, where you sail past the direct head to wind point, is easier: it is easier to judge the necessary distances from this point. It is, however, further (and therefore takes longer) and the boat has to turn through the wind.
   Aid to judging the distance: When the man overboard is lying directly abeam, then sail three boat lengths further before you turn.
2. The indirect method, where you start your approach before you reach the direct head to wind point, does save time, but it is more difficult to estimate the correct moment to turn into the wind.
   Aid to judging the distance: The correct moment to turn is immediately after gybing, or after bearing away: when the man overboard — when you have luffed up a little further — is in line with the main boom.

Windward or Lee Side Pickup
Should you approach the man so that he is on the lee side or the windward side? Opinions differ here depending on the size of the boat. Unfortunately, both have drawbacks: if the person is on the windward side and the wind is strong, the boat could easily be driven away before the crew can get hold of

him. If the person is on the lee side, however, he could easily be injured by the boat drifting over him. In the U.K., the R.Y.A. dinghy scheme recommends that the man overboard should be to windward, as this is safe and makes it easier to get him back on board again without capsizing the boat. As soon as the man or buoy makes contact with the boat at the shrouds, move up to him and the boat will look after itself.

Drift Method

By using this method you avoid the problems of going head to wind and the danger of losing track of the man. This method is possible on all boats which can be hove to.

When practising it is important to remember the following:
- The practice dummy must be weighted with some heavy object or it will not behave like a body but will drift away faster than the boat. In

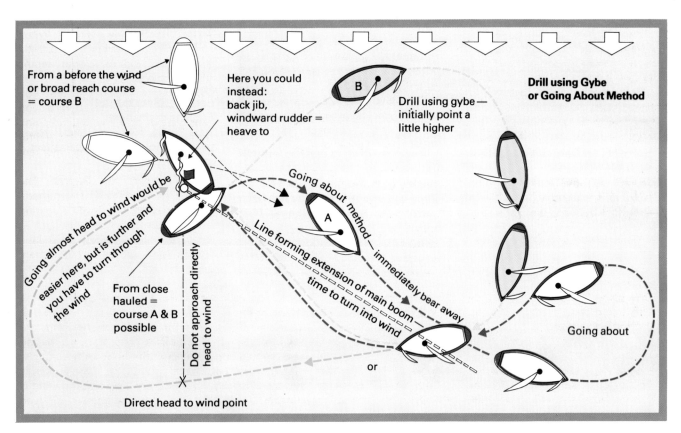

From a before the wind or broad reach course = course B

Here you could instead: back jib, windward rudder = heave to

Drill using gybe — initially point a little higher

Drill using Gybe or Going About Method

Going about method — immediately bear away

Going almost head to wind would be easier here, but is further and you have to turn through the wind

Going about

Line forming extension of main boom — time to turn into wind

From close hauled = course A & B possible

Do not approach directly head to wind

or

Direct head to wind point

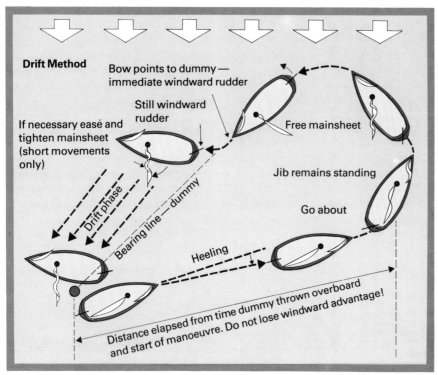

Drift Method

Bow points to dummy — immediate windward rudder

Still windward rudder

Free mainsheet

If necessary ease and tighten mainsheet (short movements only)

Drift phase

Bearing line — dummy

Jib remains standing

Go about

Heeling

Distance elapsed from time dummy thrown overboard and start of manoeuvre. Do not lose windward advantage!

lengths on a close-hauled course. When practising allow a count of about five. (If you are not on a close-hauled course, sheet in the sails and luff up till you are.) Then go about, backing the jib, ease the mainsail and bear away till the bow is pointing towards the dummy. Finally, move the rudder to windward and you will simply drift towards the dummy.

This drift phase can be well regulated — if necessary — by sheeting in and easing the mainsail as required (jib remains aback!)

> **Shouts of Command**:
> 'Man overboard!'
> (When practising count to five slowly)
> 'Ready to go about!' Reply: 'All clear!'
> 'Lee-Ho!' 'Back the jib!'
> 'Free the mainsheet!'
> (And finally if needed, and if you are not holding the mainsheet yourself:
> 'Sheet in the mainsail!' — 'Ease the mainsheet!' as necessary)

these circumstances it would be impossible to reach!

■ In very weak breezes keeping a boat hove to is extremely difficult — it is therefore better to wait for a strong breeze in which to practise this drill.

Depending on the number of seconds that elapse after the dummy has been thrown over, sail a few more boat

Rescue aids on a yacht with high topsides: hang a special rescue block and tackle on the end of the boom or use mainsheet, pull person up and swing into cockpit by pulling in the mainsheet over the guard rail.

Getting the Person back on Board

Once you have reached the person in the water and are able to grasp him, all is still not over. Actually getting the person back on board is far more difficult! If the person in the water still has his strength, then he can do most of the work himself by climbing up a ladder or by using a rope with a loop to help him climb up. On low-sided dinghies he could even climb on board over the stern or over the windward side. If, however, he is weak or even unconscious, then it is important to get him back on board as quickly as possible. On **two-man dinghies** the following method can be used:

◄ *Rescue method for one person on a small boat:*
Grasp the person like this at the stern or on the windward side (1), then lift up (2), push down again (3) and pull up and in (4 & 5).

■ Grasp the person under the arms with his back towards you on the windward side at the stern (or grip his life-jacket under the arms), then pull him up, push him down again into the water and then a big heave into the boat (see series of photographs).

By pushing him down into the water, you will produce such a good lift (aided by his life-jacket) that it is surprisingly easy to get him up and on board. On a highsided **yacht** you will have to use equipment to help you lift the person on the lee side. (The lee side is used because the heeling makes this side lower.)

The best method is to use a special block and tackle made from two double blocks (triple blocks would be better still), or the mainsheet.

■ Hook one block on to a halyard about 2 – 3 m above the deck or on the end of the raised boom, and the other on to the safety harness of the man in the water. Then pull up.

Towing and Being Towed

To approach another boat in order to tow it sail close-hauled from the lee side to a position in front of the bow of the boat and take the tow rope. Then bear away a little and stay on the same tack.

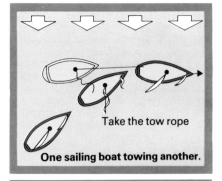

Take the tow rope

One sailing boat towing another.

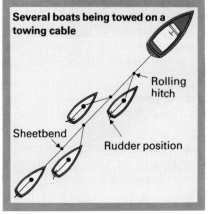

Several boats being towed on a towing cable

Rolling hitch

Sheetbend

Rudder position

Before throwing the tow rope, separate the coils into two halves holding one half only in your throwing hand.

Here the towing speed seems too fast — dangerous for non-planing boats.

■ The international signal to give if you require a tow is to swing a tow rope on the foredeck.

Prepare the tow rope in good time and belay it, take in the sail and, on dinghies, raise the centre-board by two-thirds.

> **Remember:** If you forget to raise the centre-board you could capsize!

If you do not have a strong cleat on the bow to belay the tow rope, tie it to the mast using 1½ round turns and two half hitches, or, on dinghies, also a slippery hitch so that it can be untied quickly if necessary. The length of the rope must be adjusted to ensure that both boats are sailing on the same wave phase.

When the **towing boat** starts off the tow rope must be slack to enable it to pick up speed. The last part of the rope should then be paid off slowly so that the rope gradually takes up the strain. Never pull backwards on the rope!

If you are being towed by a much larger vessel, there is a danger that you could be towed too quickly, which will damage your hull (see *Planing*) and could lead to your boat filling with water or capsizing.

Sometimes a single rope is used for towing several boats on which you can fasten your own tow rope with a rolling hitch. Remember:
1. Tie into a gap to avoid bumping other boats.
2. Secure tow rope to the mast and lead it through between shroud and forestay (starboard side for port boards, and vice versa).
3. The last boat uses a sheetbend to tie his rope to the main towing rope.

Anchoring

Anchorage

A suitable anchorage which fulfils certain conditions is essential. The following must be borne in mind:
■ Look for a good anchoring spot. Sand is good; stony and overgrown or weedy spots are bad.
■ Take into account the depth of the water, the draft of your boat and the state of the tide.
■ The distance between anchored yachts must be such that each yacht can turn in a circle round its anchor.
■ The anchorage must be well protected from wind and waves.
■ It is dangerous to anchor your boat on a *lee-shore*, i.e. when your yacht could be blown on to land by an on-shore wind. And if in doubt buoy your anchor.
■ Never drop anchor in a navigable channel.

Anchoring

As soon as you have found your spot, you can begin the anchoring procedure:
1. First of all the jib is taken in (rolled up) to make room for the preparations on the foredeck.
2. The anchor chain (or warp and chain) is arranged in coils on deck and secured to the anchor.
3. While the anchor is held over the side — ready to drop — (or hung on the bow roller) luff up into the anchorage (in a current, turn against the current).

4. The anchor is slowly lowered to the sea-bed but not until the boat begins to drift astern. Remember: never let the chain simply rush out all at once or throw the anchor overboard! Never drop anchor when the boat is standing still or the chain could become tangled. In light breezes you could encourage the anchor to dig in by using the engine to make sternway.

5. The length of the anchor chain should be at least three times, or better still five times (or more), the depth of the water, depending on the wind strength, the waves and the proximity of the shore, and the chain should be well belayed to the cleat (samson post) at the bow.

6. The mainsail is taken in, and the anchor is checked to see if it is holding. Have a look at permanent landmarks abeam of your boat and notice if your boat is moving in relation to them.

Shouts of Command:
'Prepare to take in the foresail!'
('Prepare the jib halyard!')
Reply: 'Ready to take in the jib!'
('Jib halyard ready!')
'Take in jib!'
'Prepare anchor!'
Reply: 'Anchor ready!'
'Prepare to drop anchor!'
Reply: 'Anchor ready to drop!'
'Drop anchor!'
Reply: 'Anchor dropped!'
(The commands to take in the mainsail follow)

Weighing Anchor

This procedure is similar to the manoeuvre used when casting off from a buoy. First of all you have to take any neighbouring boats into account, and decide whether there is enough room to go to leeward to pick up speed, and also which is the best side to sail away on.

The manoeuvre step by step is as follows:

1. Hoist the mainsail and prepare jib to hoist (or hoist the jib as well and furl).

2. *Short scope* the anchor — pull in the chain till it is almost perpendicular (without moving the anchor).

3. Swing the boat round to the side (back the mainsail) and then haul the anchor up.

4. Immediately, hoist or unfurl the jib and hold it aback, so that the boat can bear away quickly and pick up speed.

5. Pull anchor on board, clean and stow away.

Shouts of Command:
(Commands to hoist sail)
'Prepare to weigh anchor!'
Reply: 'All clear!'
'Short scope the anchor!'
Reply: 'Anchor is up and down!'
'Up anchor!'
Reply: 'Anchor is free!'
'Unfurl the jib!'
'Back the jib to starboard/port!'

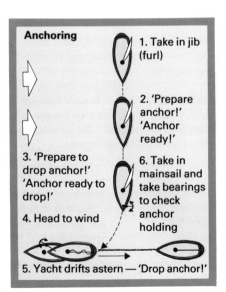

Anchoring

1. Take in jib (furl)

2. 'Prepare anchor!' 'Anchor ready!'

3. 'Prepare to drop anchor!' 'Anchor ready to drop!'

4. Head to wind

5. Yacht drifts astern — 'Drop anchor!'

6. Take in mainsail and take bearings to check anchor holding

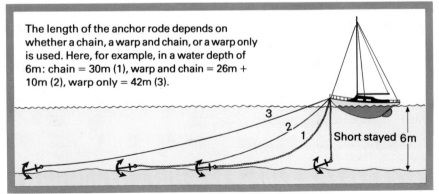

The length of the anchor rode depends on whether a chain, a warp and chain, or a warp only is used. Here, for example, in a water depth of 6m: chain = 30m (1), warp and chain = 26m + 10m (2), warp only = 42m (3).

Short stayed 6m

Capsizing

A dinghy will usually capsize to leeward, and sometimes, but not often, to the windward side. An inexperienced sailor may have to cope with this situation many times, but a good sailor should hardly ever capsize. Knowing what to do if your boat capsizes, and how to right it again, is an important part of sailing technique.

Causes of a capsize to leeward
- Bad gybing technique when wind is too strong.
- No counter-rudder or given too late in a gust on a broad reach. The boat luffs up (loses speed, stability decreases, centrifugal force).
- Luffing up too late and too far in a gust on a close-hauled course (loses speed and stability).

Causes of a capsize to windward
- On a close-hauled course a sudden strong adverse wind shift; the crew, sitting out, cannot get back into the boat fast enough to bear away.
- Rolling too much before the wind.
- Gust suddenly subsides and crew, who are sitting out (or using trapeze) cannot get back into the boat fast enough.

1 A normal capsize for conditions such as this and with this type of boat (Laser) which should pose no problems.
2 Important: Immediately climb on centre-board.
3 Do not take a breather on the side of the boat...
4 ... or you will have a complete inversion on your hands!

- Crew sits out and mainsheet eased too quickly.

Righting the Boat

A capsize is no problem on modern planing dinghies so long as the correct technique is used to right the boat and it has sufficient buoyancy:
- Climb on to the centre-board and pull the dinghy up again.

If on a two-man dinghy there is only room for one on the centre-board, the other man can help by swimming to the mast head (wear a life-jacket!) and pushing it up. If the crew has fallen in the water it is important not to lose contact with the boat; tie a line (fore-line, sheet) to the boat to prevent it drifting away. If mast and sail are pointing to windward (the boat has capsized to windward), you will have to turn the bow into the wind before trying to right it.

> **Tip:** The procedure described in many books of turning the bow by swimming in the direction of the wind is hardly practicable. It is better to stand on the centre-board and rock up and down, till the wind catches underneath the mainsail and pushes the boat round.

Always remove the sheets from the cleats (if they were cleated) before righting the boat so the sail can blow free and the boat will stand still. A completely inverted dinghy (mast pointing downwards) can be brought up to a horizontal position — if pulling

If pulling on the centre-board is not enough to right the dinghy then you should attach a line (mainsheet) like this. By doing this you increase the leverage.

This is the basic position for righting a capsize: immediately climb on centre-board, hold the edge of the deck (or deck band) and lean back.

on the centre-board does not work — by climbing on the hull, hauling the sheet or another line over the side of the boat and pulling on it.

Many modern planing dinghies are constructed so the cockpit empties itself while being righted. However, if this is not so and you have a *self-bailer valve* you should bear away on a broad reach if possible (if you have enough room leewards) so the water empties

Climbing in early as the boat rights itself is very important to avoid a capsize to the other side. This photograph shows the correct procedure.

as you increase speed. Failing this, use a bailer or plastic bucket to bail out.

When You Need Help

If your dinghy does not have enough buoyancy and has therefore filled up (e.g. wooden Pirate) you will definitely need a tow. The following procedure should be followed for safety reasons:

If you right your boat by pushing the mast up or pulling on the centre-board in the water, you must always hold a line attached to the boat to prevent it from drifting away.

- Make sure that everyone is all right and if necessary give first aid.
- Do not swim away from the boat to the shore since you are more clearly visible close to your boat. Also you will not stand a chance in a heavy swell fully dressed.
- Keep your clothes on as they will lessen your chances of suffering from exposure. The weight will feel awkward in the water but it will not affect your buoyancy.
- If you cannot see any help close by, sit on the capsized boat and raise and lower your arms above your head to attract attention.
- Prevent a complete inversion by holding the centre-board.
- When help arrives, take in the sails, right the boat and secure the tow rope to the mast at deck height.
- If the crew are not too tired it is a good idea to help the towing boat by steering with it.

Typical mistakes made by beginners:
- *Climbing on centre-board too late — crew falls in the water or dinghy inverts.*
- *Climbing on the high side of the boat — dinghy inverts.*
- *Righting the boat from the water without attaching a line — dinghy drifts away.*
- *Righting boat without freeing sheet — dinghy capsizes again.*
- *Climbing on board a righted dinghy too late — another capsize, to the other side this time!*

What to Do in Strong Winds and Storms

Unexpected thunderstorms can be very dangerous to the sailor since they can be extremely violent. You should therefore keep a constant eye on the weather whenever you are sailing. If you see signs of an approaching thunderstorm (large anvil-shaped or black-edged clouds — especially when they come from the south-west) you should immediately sail for 'home', and if you are thinking of embarking on a sailing expedition, forget it!

Do not rely solely on storm warnings, but use your transistor radio and your common sense and act quickly if you see signs of an approaching thunderstorm. Three things must be done if you see storm clouds gathering, if the wind suddenly increases or if there is a storm warning:

1. The crew wears **life-jackets**.
2. **Reef** the sails. Most dinghies can be reefed. Take in the mainsail first, to give you room to handle the jib.
3. The boat itself (especially important for yachts) must be **kept away** from the shore the wind is blowing onto unless the harbour can be reached.

Weathering the Storm

If, however, you find yourself taken by surprise you will have to weather the storm. On a dinghy there is only one thing you can do and that is to take in all the sails. On a yacht, however, you can do the following:

In a stormy SW wind like this you should know how to weather a squall. You should never venture too far out alone or you may not be seen if you get into difficulties.

1. Weather the storm by reefing all sails (or hoisting storm sails) avoiding if possible running before the wind.
2. Heave to with storm sails hoisted (see also p.76).
3. Run before the wind without sails — this is called running under bare poles. This is only possible if you have room to leeward. Drop anchor before you are driven aground on the shore.
4. Take in sails and use your engine to take you slowly diagonally across the waves.

Weathering a Squall

Every experienced helmsman must know how to weather strong gusts of wind, otherwise he may find his dinghy capsizing. On a yacht the rigging could be badly damaged. An approaching gust (increase in speed of the true wind) can be recognised by a fast rippling over the surface of the water.

On a close-hauled course there are three things you can do:
- Luff up.
- Ease the mainsheet.
- Sit out as far as possible.

When going to windward, you must be careful that this is done exactly at the right moment, or you will merely increase the heeling and this could lead to a capsize. When easing the sheet, by hand if possible, you should not simply let it run out, but ease it very gently, and tighten up again as soon as possible to retain momentum. Experienced sailors have a trick which they can use in heavy squalls: they sail 'on the edge of the wind', i.e. they luff up very high and sail close to the wind so that only half of the wind force hits the sail. This counteracts the heeling momentum of the squall, and the boat can be kept upright.

> **Tip**: If there is a danger of capsizing, raise the centre-board a little to reduce heeling.

On a **broad reach** it would be wrong to luff up; instead you should ease the sheets and sit out. Counter-rudder should also be given to prevent an involuntary luffing up and turning moment (and a loss of speed and stability).

On a **run** the boat will tend to carry weather helm and this must be counteracted by careful counter-rudder (not too much or you risk an involuntary gybe!). It is better, however, to stay away from this course altogether in strong winds.

Reefing

Reefing means decreasing the area of sail and is a basic safety measure (taking pressure off the rigging) used in strong winds. However, there are also sound technical reasons for reefing: the boat will heel less, carry less weather helm and therefore sail better (centre of effort moves downwards and forwards). Except on dinghies, you decrease the sail area by reefing the mainsail and exchanging the jib for a smaller one. Modern racing sailors will always reef the mainsail first in order to counteract the weather helm produced by heeling. The jib is then taken down and a smaller one hoisted.

How to Reef

There are two basic ways of reefing:
- Reefing by rolling the sail (roll reef).
- Reefing by tying the sail (points reef).

For the **roll reef** method, the mainsail is rolled round the boom, the boom being turned by means of a ratchet or sliding gooseneck. To do this, one man has to turn, a second has to reef and a third has to pull the leech towards the end of the boom and also remove the lower sail batten. To enable the boom to be turned, the mainsheet must be attached to a free-turning fitting on the boom end or led through a sheet ring.

For the **points reef** method, the mainsail usually has two rows of small eyelets, *reefing points* (see diagram for *mainsail*, p.19), through which the *reefing ties* or *reef line* are fed. The boat

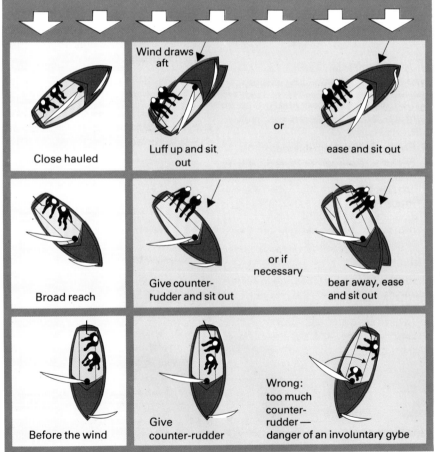

Close hauled

Wind draws aft

Luff up and sit out

or

ease and sit out

Broad reach

Give counter-rudder and sit out

or if necessary

bear away, ease and sit out

Before the wind

Give counter-rudder

Wrong: too much counter-rudder— danger of an involuntary gybe

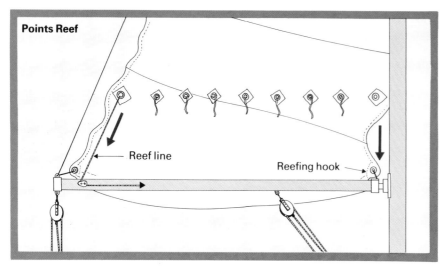

Points Reef

Reef line

Reefing hook

■ The kicking strap can be used.

It is important to have at least three reefing positions in all sails of cruising and racing boats.

Reefing on a Dinghy

As a rule dinghies do not have any reefing equipment. Reefing is done by removing the boom from the mast at the gooseneck; then the sail is rolled by hand round the boom (in harbour if possible). It is vital that the mainsheet is secured to a reefing claw (or reefing carriage)(see also p.22). Many modern dinghies use centre mainsheets, making it impossible to reef at all.

is lying hove to, and the main halyard is eased until the first *reef cringle* reaches the special hook on the boom. Then the aftermost *reef line* is pulled tight. The loose cloth under the boom is now tied up by means of the reefing ties (or reef line).

Advantages and Disadvantages

The points reef system is preferred by modern racing sailors. It is also used by cruising yachtsmen since it has definite advantages over the roll reef method:

■ Sail is not dragged and pulled so much, and is therefore less likely to be damaged.
■ Better sail profile retained.
■ Fewer crew members required to reef.
■ Can be used with any type of sheet fittings.
■ The lower sail batten need not be removed, and the main boom therefore does not sink aft.

When using the roll reef method one man eases the main halyard, and the other turns the boom with the handle.

Mainsail rolled up — it is possible to roll to any point.

When using the points reef method the loose cloth is tied up by the reefing ties.

Sea Damage and Running Aground

Sea Damage

Damage which happens to a boat because of a storm, collision, or running aground, is called *sea damage*. This is usually caused by bad weather conditions, strong gusts and storms. The best precautionary measure which can be taken is to ensure that all equipment is in good order. A good sailor, before setting off — especially on a rented boat — will always check his equipment. Are the shrouds correctly tensioned? Are the sheets safe (are they worn through)? Will the halyards hold, etc? If sea damage occurs, you should try to ensure that as little further damage as possible is done, and that you can get 'home' safely.

If the sail tears: luff up immediately and take in the torn sail. Remember: do this even if the tear is very small as it will quickly get bigger! If the tear is near the foot the strain can be taken off it by reefing the sail.

If the mast breaks: get the broken parts of the mast back on board. Remove the sail. Remove standing and running gear. If you cannot bring the broken parts aboard use fenders to protect the hull and lash the spars securely. The main boom or spinnaker boom may be used as a makeshift mast.

If a shroud breaks: the windward shroud is always the one to break! If the mast does not break, ease the sheets

immediately and then go about. You will be able to sail on the other tack. It may be possible to fasten a rope or halyard to the broken shroud and to tie this to the chainplate. It is a good idea to keep a metal jam cleat or a bulldog clip in your tool box: you can use them to make an eye in the broken end of the shroud.

If the forestay breaks: the luff of the jib can replace the forestay. There should be no problem as long as you have a jib hoisted. If not, sail immediately before the wind and shackle the jib halyard (spinnaker halyard) to the bow and cleat.

If the backstay breaks: this will usually happen on a run when a spinnaker is being used. Take in the spinnaker immediately and take a close-hauled course. Use a spare halyard or the topping left as a temporary backstay.

A break in the running rigging: so long as a halyard is not broken at a point where it runs over a roller, it can be tied together (or spliced). If not, then you must use a spare halyard — or sail on with the other sail only. The mainsheet cannot be knotted since it runs through blocks. It is a good idea to have a spare line on board which can be used as a mainsheet.

If the rudder breaks: try to make a temporary rudder (paddle, board). If necessary steer using the sails only; going to windward — tighter mainsail and slacker jib; going to leeward — tighter jib and slacker mainsail.

If the tiller breaks: use paddle or boat hook. Otherwise as for rudder damage.

If the main boom breaks: rig the mainsheet on a stern cleat and sail loose-footed.

Leak: this can happen if you run aground or are involved in a collision. A very small leak can be stopped with a handkerchief, sailbag or similar. For a larger leak you could use a cushion, pillow, or inflatable life-jacket; press it into place using a plank. A 'collision mat' could be used on the outside of the leak, i.e. a jib is pulled under the boat from the bow and secured to starboard and port so that it presses up against the leak.

If the leak is high enough up you should try to keep it above water by making the boat heel.

If all else fails, bail out and try to reach the nearest shore. Failing this you will find yourself in a similar situation to that of a capsized dinghy.

If possible a yacht should be taken into shallow water before it goes down (mark the spot with buoys!).

> **Remember:** Swim away from a sinking yacht to avoid being sucked under. There is also a danger of being caught up in the rigging and pulled under.

Running Aground

When a dinghy touches the bottom there should be no problem since all you need do is raise the centre-board and perhaps also the rudder a little. If necessary climb out and give a gentle

Stranded! During a stormy night this yacht was driven onto a lee shore.

Currents

It is important to know how to handle currents especially if you are sailing on rivers and in tidal coastal areas. You can tell in which direction the current is flowing by looking at buoys, boats at anchor or those moored to buoys. You can determine the strength of the current by looking at the diagonal position of marker buoys and the eddies caused by them. Remember also that the current is always stronger in deep water (centre of the river) than in shallow water.

For our purposes there are two types of currents:

push. On inshore waters the keel of a yacht can easily touch ground but this does not usually do any damage; the outcome depends for the most part which course you are on!

On a **close-hauled** course there is less danger of the wind pushing you further aground and therefore the following steps, if taken immediately, are usually enough:
Free mainsail, hold jib aback, heel the boat to lee by moving weight over, push bow away using boathook. If necessary sheet in the mainsail to increase heeling.

On a **broad reach** or a **run** the yacht will be driven further aground. You should immediately ease the sheets and then take in the sails. An anchor can be taken out to the windward side if you have a tender.

To get free the draught has to be reduced and this is done by making the boat heel, moving the crew's weight aft, or, if necessary, by unloading to reduce the weight.

The following are ways of making the boat heel effectively:
■ The crew hangs onto the shrouds.
■ Crew hangs on the boom, or the tender is swung out and some of the crew jump in. (Beware of breaking the boom!)

If you do not succeed in freeing the heeling boat by starting the engine or getting out and pushing, *kedging* is the only remedy left. This involves using an anchor to haul the boat free. If need be you will have to get help. After going aground you must immediately examine the hull to make sure it is undamaged and is still watertight.

1. The current flowing with or directly against your course: the effect of this current is simply to slow you down or speed you up; it will not have any effect on your direction. If the current is with the boat the speed will increase by the speed of the current. However, if the current is against it, it will be slowed down by that amount. The **speed through the water** is the speed shown by the log in relation to the water flowing past. The **speed over the bottom** is the speed in relation to the river-bed (or sea-bed).

2. The current flowing at an angle to your course causing **current drift**: a current coming from directly abeam causes the most drift.

You have to ensure that you keep to a **course over the bottom** rather than a **course through the water** to reach your

Negotiating a narrow entrance with a current (wind direction and sail position excluded here): Boat A is crossing the current, Boat B is going with the current and Boat C is against the current.
The current will sweep A downstream, as in A1, so it has to point upstream enough to travel across on a direct course.

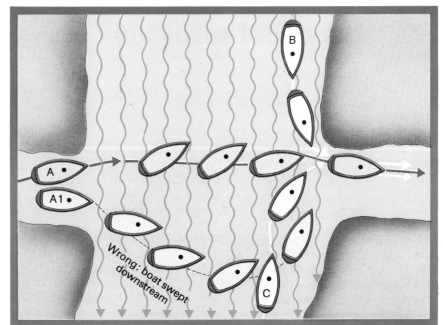

goal. In other words: you constantly have to counteract the current to prevent the boat from being deflected off the desired course.

Some basic points:
- In a strong current point the boat into the current when you moor up.
- Lower anchor pointing into the current.
- In a current running across a harbour entrance, keep to the upstream side of the entrance (but keep well away from the harbour wall to prevent the stern colliding with it when the current pushes the bow downstream).
- When manoeuvring in a harbour with a current, keep the anchor ready at all times.

Approaching the jetty with the current: Boat A has gone head to wind but thinks it is not going to be able to stop in time; therefore, in position 2 it throws over its bow anchor to stop itself. The current then turns the boat to position 4 and by easing the anchor line, the boat will drift into its mooring. Boat B goes with the current alongside the jetty, securing its sternline first (3) so that the stern is not pulled round by the current. (This should only be attempted in weak currents.)

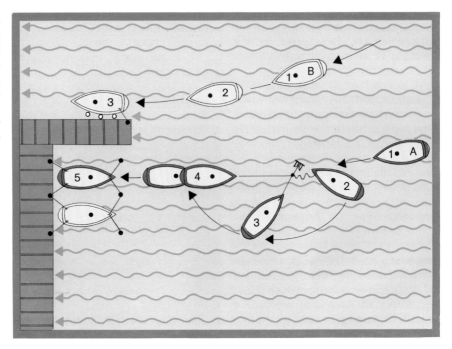

5 Basic Meteorology

Highs and Lows

The weather depends on temperature, air pressure and humidity. The air warmed by the earth's surface expands, especially upwards. The air mass lying above the surface of the earth is reduced, the air pressure decreases and an *area of low pressure* (shortened to *low*) develops. Similarly, a mass of cooled air, which is heavier than warm air, sinks down to the earth's surface, resulting in an *area of high pressure* (shortened to *high*).

■ A low is formed when part of the earth's surface warms up more quickly than the surrounding areas.

■ A high is formed when part of the earth's surface is cooled down more than the surrounding areas.

This results in a difference in air pressure between the two places, with the different pressures constantly trying to even each other out. The resulting horizontal air movement as the air from the high pressure area flows into the low pressure area is the wind. If a high and a low are close together, there is a large difference in air pressure which results in strong to gale-force winds. On weather maps all the places with the same air pressure are joined by *isobars*.

The air pressure gradient is shown by the closeness of the isobars which are charted at five-millibar intervals.

■ If the lines are close together, the pressure gradient is large, so the wind will be strong.

■ If the isobars are well spaced, there will be a small pressure gradient which means gentle breezes.

The isobars of a high, moving outwards from the centre, show falling air pressure; those of a low show rising pressure.

Because of the earth's rotation, the wind spirals anti-clockwise into a low in the northern hemisphere, and clockwise in the southern hemisphere. The wind spirals clockwise out of a high in the northern hemisphere and anti-clockwise in the southern hemisphere.

The air pressure, which is on average 1013 millibars (or 760mm) at sea level, can be read off on a barometer, and we can reach certain conclusions when we see the pressure changing:

■ A low will move towards the area where the air pressure is falling rapidly.

■ A high will move towards the area where the air pressure is climbing quickly.

■ In an area where the air pressure is constant or rising slowly, a period of good weather can be expected.

■ Air pressure which is steadily falling indicates bad weather.

■ Air pressure which is falling fast means there is a danger of storms.

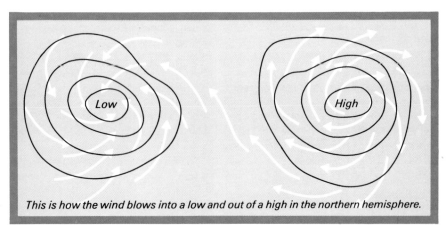

This is how the wind blows into a low and out of a high in the northern hemisphere.

Thermal Winds, Thunderstorms, Wind Speeds

Land and Sea Breezes

Thermal winds are local winds pro duced by the effect of the sun's rays on the water and land.

Because land will warm up more quickly than water, in sunny weather a small low will form over the land, into which the wind will flow from the water.

- The **sea breeze**, an on-shore wind which blows from the sea on to the land, is produced as the land warms up, usually after midday.

The opposite is true in the evening: the land cools faster than the water, resulting in a small thermal high over the land and a thermal low over the water. The wind blows into the low and

- produces the off-shore **land breeze**.

These winds can be very strong, especially in mountainous areas.

Thunderstorms

It is possible to distinguish between the *frontal storm* produced on a cold front of a large low and the *summer storm* which is confined to one particular area. The sailor is mainly concerned with summer storms which usually occur in the afternoon.

Sudden updraughts of damp, warm air result in showers of rain, even hail and

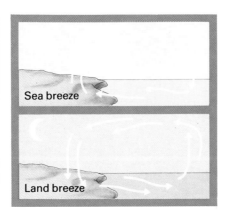

Sea breeze

Land breeze

snow, and also cause electrical discharges. If the potential difference between the charged air layers is sufficiently great, then lightning is produced.

You can calculate how far away a storm is by counting the seconds between the lightning and the first clap of thunder and dividing by three. This will give an approximate distance in kilometres.

How can you recognise the signs of an approaching thunderstorm?

Usually a thunderstorm will build up in the south-west, and if a sailor notices large clouds (cumulus) gathering in that direction, this is his first warning. These threatening thunder clouds are not always easily recognised as they can sometimes be masked by wispy clouds. If you notice a dark cloud edge getting nearer, you should be prepared for a thunderstorm. It is impossible to know at the time whether the storm will actually hit you or blow over. A special feature of a gathering thunderstorm is the suction wind. If the storm produces a small low pressure area, this will attract the wind into it: a sudden squall with then follow. If, for example, the prevailing wind is blowing from the SW

and a thunderstorm is approaching from the same direction, after a short period of calm (first calm) the wind will swing round to the north-east. As the thunderstorm gets nearer the squall will set in from the SW, usually after a second lull (lull before the storm!) caused by the updraught before the wind turns. If, however, the wind is coming from the NE and the thunderstorm is building up in the SW, there will be no first calm. The wind will freshen up and the first gusts will appear after the short calm before the storm.

One often hears inexperienced sailors saying 'the thunderstorm seemed to come from nowhere' or 'the thunderstorm was on me in less than no time at all'. Those who use such expressions are either rather stupid or extremely gullible. It is true that a thunderstorm can build up very quickly, and the first gusts can hit you suddenly, but the signs are always recognisable a long time in advance — when the storm clouds begin to gather and the sky darkens. (See also chapter *What to do in Strong Winds and Storms.*)

Storm Warnings

Many sailing areas have a storm warning system which each and every sailor must be aware of. If you are about to sail on unknown waters you have a clear duty to find out about the local warning system. Today the warning is usually given in radio broadcasts and by hoisting a black conical signal at coastguard stations:

- Point uppermost — gale from northerly sector.

■ Point down — gale from southerly sector.

The Beaufort Wind Scale

The wind strength is the same as the average air speed, usually measured in metres per second or in nautical miles per hour (knots).

The Beaufort Scale divides the wind speed into twelve strengths and gives a short description of the effect of the wind on water and land for each one. The scale is not linear, i.e. there is a bigger jump between the wind speeds in each class the higher up the scale you go.

Beaufort Number	Description	Wind Speed m/s	km/h	Knots	Effects on Sea and Land
0	Calm	0 – 0.2	< 1	< 1	Sea flat and calm. Smoke rises vertically.
1	Light vespers	0.3– 1.5	1–5	1–3	Ripples similar to fish scales. Smoke moves. Vessels just have steerage way.
2	Light breeze	1.6– 3.3	6–11	4–6	Small wavelets. Crests have a glassy sheen. Leaves stir, flags stir.
3	Gentle breeze	3.4– 5.4	12–19	7–10	Crests begin to break. Occasional scattered small white horses. Leaves and twigs are in constant motion, flags extend.
4	Moderate breeze	5.5– 7.9	20–28	11–15	Waves becoming longer, fairly frequent white horses. Dust and paper lifted up, twigs move.
5	Fresh breeze	8–10.7	29–38	16–21	Plenty of breaking crests. Small trees sway, flags crack resoundingly.
6	Strong breeze	10.8–13.8	39–49	22–27	Large waves, foaming crests, spray. Telegraph wires whistle, large branches in motion.
7	Near gale	13.9–17.1	50–61	28–33	Heaping seas, foam from breaking crests blown downwind. Difficulty felt when walking against gusts.
8	Gale	17.2–20.7	62–74	34–40	Large waves with long deep troughs, foam blown from crests. Branches break off trees, walking difficult.
9	Strong gale	20.8–24.4	75–88	41–47	High waves, dense streaks of foam. Crests of waves break. Slight structural damage may occur.
10	Storm	24.5–28.4	89–102	48–55	Very high waves with overhanging crests. Patches of foam whipped up so that sea takes on a frothing appearance. Breaking seas become heavy and visibility is affected. Trees may be uprooted.
11	Violent storm	28.5–32.6	103–117	56–63	Exceptionally high waves. Whole surface of sea hidden in foam blown downwind. Serious storm damage.
12	Hurricane	> 32.6	> 117	> 63	Air filled with driving foam. Sea completely white. Worst possible damage.

6 Racing

Regattas — Races — Marking — Course

A regatta usually consists of several races carried out on one day or over several days.

Racing rules come into force five minutes before the start, with the preparatory signal, and finish when all boats have crossed the finishing line (or if the race has been stopped officially).

There are three different scoring systems; the club short series, the club long series, and the Olympic, as follows:

Finishing position	Short	Long	Olympic
1	¾	0	0
2	2	3	3
3	3	5.7	5.7
4	4	8	8
5	5	10	10
6	6	11.7	11.7
7	7	Place + 6 = 13	Place + 6 = 13
8	8	etc.	etc.

Races are run under the I.Y.R.U. (International Yacht Racing Union) racing rules with modifications by the Nautical Authority (the Royal Yachting Association in the U.K.). The regulations are revised every four years after the Olympic Games.

Before the start of every race the helmsman receives racing instructions which outline the race regulations, time and place of the start, courses and a list of competitors.

In order to take part in competitive racing you will need a valid measurement certificate for your boat. The helmsman must also be a member of a sailing club.

Course

As a rule the so-called *Olympic Course* is sailed. This is a three-sided course marked out by buoys which includes tacking, broad reaching and running legs.

If a green flag is hoisted you must leave the buoys to starboard. If the red flag is hoisted you must leave them to port. The entire course is therefore: Start—1—2—3—1—3—finish.

Immediately after the starting signal has been given you will usually have to contend with sailing against the wind, which means tacking up to Buoy 1. You will have a broad reach course on a starboard and port tack up to Buoys 2 and 3. The route from Buoy 1 back to 3 is a run. You will always have to tack to the finish. On most inland waters, because of lack of space, another triangle is usually sailed — Start—1—2—3—1—3—1—2—3—finish. (A shortened course would be Start—1—2—3—1—3—finish or Start—1—2—3—1—2—3—finish.)

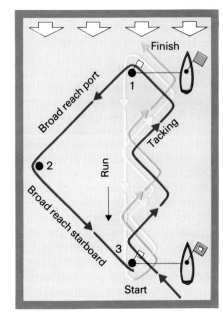

Start — Finish — Important Concepts

Start and Finish

The starting and finishing lines are marked by two buoys, or by one buoy (often Buoy 3 at the start and Buoy 1 at the finish), and the starting or finishing boat. Ten minutes before the starting time laid down in the programme the **warning signal**, usually the class flag, is hoisted. At the same time a sound signal (usually a gun) is made to draw attention to the flag. Five minutes later there is a **preparatory signal** and the flag 'P' of the international flag alphabet (the *Blue Peter*) is hoisted; it means 'I am about to sail'. From this moment the racing rules are in force.

At the start the **class flag** is lowered. Flag 'P' may remain flying if subsequent classes are starting at five-minute intervals, but it is usually dipped and hoisted immediately. Boats crossing the line too early are recalled (**individual recall**: flag 'X' or class flag at the dip) and they must cross the starting line again without hindering the others in any way. If several boats cross the line too early, the start may be repeated for everyone (**general recall**: First Substitute Pennant). In order to avoid further false starts a **one minute rule** may be brought into force (flag 'I'). This states that a yacht will be disqualified if in the last minute before the start it crosses the line. However, the sailing instructions sometimes permit offenders to sail into a starting position over a line forming an extension of the starting line (**round the ends rule**). See

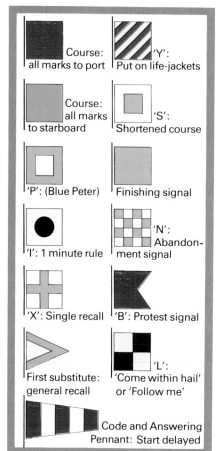

Course: all marks to port	'Y': Put on life-jackets
Course: all marks to starboard	'S': Shortened course
'P': (Blue Peter)	Finishing signal
'I': 1 minute rule	'N': Abandonment signal
'X': Single recall	'B': Protest signal
First substitute: general recall	'L': 'Come within hail' or 'Follow me'
Code and Answering Pennant: Start delayed	

diagram for flags commonly used in races.

A blue flag is hoisted on the finishing boat. A boat is said to have finished the race when it has crossed the finishing line with any part of its hull, equipment or crew, in their normal position, from the direction of the last mark.

Important Concepts

Proper Course

A proper course is any course taken by a yacht **after** the starting signal to reach the finishing line before the other competitors.

Clear Astern — Clear Ahead — Overlapping

A boat is clear astern of another when its hull (including all equipment in normal position) is behind an imaginary line running across the most aft point on the hull (or the equipment in normal position) of the other boat. The other boat is therefore clear ahead.

Boat A is clear astern of B, C overlaps D, and G seems clear astern of E, although there is an overlap since F is between and overlapping both.

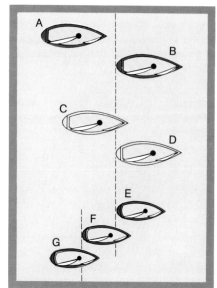

Rights of Way

The same rules apply here as to non-racing sailors.
A short reminder:
■ A yacht tacking to port shall keep clear of a yacht tacking to starboard.
■ A windward yacht shall keep clear of a leeward yacht.
■ The overtaking yacht must give way.

The overtaking rule applies until there is an overlap, which can be to lee or windward. If you overtake on the **windward** side, the boat being overtaken can hinder the overtaking boat by luffing up. The lee boat ahead may luff up until the overtaking boat has reached a point where the helmsman is sitting at a point abeam of the lee boat's mast. The helmsman should call 'Mast abeam!' and the lee yacht should then bear away on to its original course (see diagram).

When overtaking on the lee side the boat ahead, after an overlap has been established, becomes the windward yacht and must keep clear. The yacht overtaking to lee, however, must allow the windward yacht enough room and opportunity to keep clear, i.e. he cannot luff up above his proper course.

Remember: A boat in a race must observe the right of way rules if he meets a non-racing boat. You should, however, be fair and try not to get in the way of racing yachts.

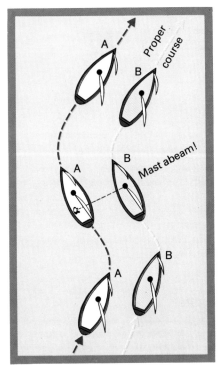

B is overtaken by A and may luff up till A is in 'mast abeam' position. B must then bear away again on the proper course.

Going About and Gybing

A yacht going about or gybing must keep clear of other yachts. A yacht is said to be tacking from the moment it turns through the wind until is is pointing in the direction of its next chosen course. A yacht is said to be gybing from when the mainsail foot crosses the midships axis as it turns away from the wind to the time it is on its next chosen course. If two yachts are going about or gybing at the same time, the yacht on the port side must keep clear.

Rounding the Course Marks

The course marks must be rounded on the prescribed side and must not be touched. If a yacht touches a mark and it is that yacht's fault, i.e. by rounding it badly, she must sail round it again correctly. If the buoy is on the starboard side the yacht must execute a correct rounding clockwise and vice versa to port.

If two or more yachts wish to round a mark (after the start!) the yacht which is on the inside has right of way if, two yacht lengths before the mark, she has an overlap on the outside yacht.

If both boats are sailing on different tacks, the rule 'starboard before port tack' applies.

Boat A is in the inside position and there is an overlap. B and C must allow A room to round the mark.

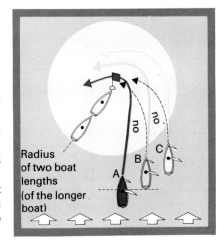

Terminology used for official Government and National Authority Publications

Vessel: includes vessels for use both on lakes and inland waterways including small vessels and ferries and any floating equipment.

Small vessel: vessel with displacement less than 15t, amphibious vessels, air beds, sea-landing aircraft; (excluding tug-boats, ferries).

Underway: any vessel, floating body or installation is said to be underway if it is not at anchor, secured to land or aground.

Night: the time between sunset and sunrise.

Day: the time between sunrise and sunset.

Short Blast: a blast lasting about one second.

Long Blast: a blast lasting about four seconds.

Master

Every vessel must have a *master* on board who is wholly responsible both for the boat and the crew, and who must be suitable both physically and mentally, and experienced. The master may allow a *helmsman* to steer the vessel, but the master is still responsible for the vessel's safety.

Rules and Regulations

1 Pleasure boats, yachts and dinghies should observe the following rules for their own safety:
- Overtake only if there is sufficient sea room.
- You should only overtake if you are sure it is safe.
- Course and speed should be maintained in such a way as to prevent collision.

2 There are additional rules applicable to **small vessels**:
- Small vessels must give way to large vessels in a navigable channel.
- Small powered vessels must keep clear of unpowered vessels.
- Small vessels without an engine (e.g. rowing boats) should give way to sailing vessels (but in practice, sailing boats usually give way first).
- Small vessels with a duty to give way who meet another vessel head-on must turn to starboard in good time. If this is not possible they must indicate clearly and in good time what their intentions are (give a sound signal).

3 **Small vessels under sail** should give way as follows when meeting or

Some customary positions for boat name etc.

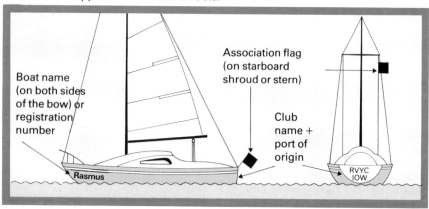

Boat name (on both sides of the bow) or registration number

Rasmus

Association flag (on starboard shroud or stern)

Club name + port of origin

RVYC IOW

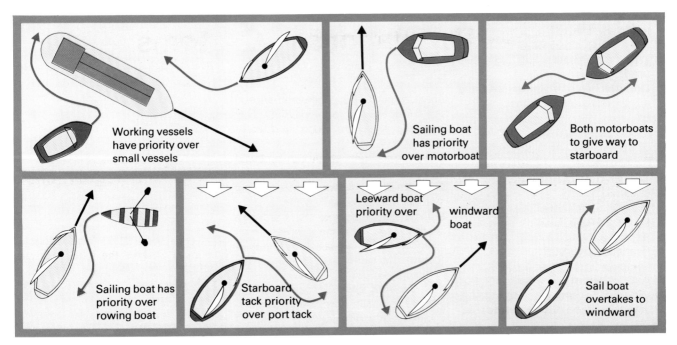

Working vessels have priority over small vessels

Sailing boat has priority over motorboat

Both motorboats to give way to starboard

Sailing boat has priority over rowing boat

Starboard tack priority over port tack

Leeward boat priority over windward boat

Sail boat overtakes to windward

overtaking another vessel:

■ When each has the wind on a different side, the vessel which has the wind on the port side shall keep out of the way of the other.

■ When both have the wind on the same side, the vessel which is to windward shall keep out of the way of the vessel which is to leeward.

■ A sailing vessel may overtake another sailing vessel on the windward side, but it is often courteous to pass to leeward.

4 **Danger from wake and waves**: a boat must restrict its speed so that it causes no damage or inconvenience to moored boats, sailing boats and other water users. Speed must be reduced (so that the boat can be steered safely):

■ At harbour entrances.

The most important give-way rules

Common situation when sailing: boats on different tacks on a collision course. The boat on the right with no. 9 on the bow is on a port tack and must give way.

The rule which states that a rowing boat (small vessel without motor) must give way to a sail boat is problematical: in a good wind a sail boat is much more powerful than a rowing boat; also people in a rowing boat are often inexperienced and have never heard of give-way rules. In other words — be fair and give way voluntarily!

- In the vicinity of moorings and moored vessels.
- Near ferries.
- When sailing past floating pontoons used by clubs.
- On stretches of water where there are speed restriction signs.

5 **Do not anchor or moor:**
- In shipping lanes, lock canals and narrow waters.
- At the mouth of a navigable estuary or canal.
- At harbour entrances.
- In the path of a ferry.
- Anywhere which would obstruct a floating bridge, etc.
- Under bridges.
- At busy commercial quays.
- Where signs prohibit mooring, e.g. at the steps of a busy quayside.

6 **Waterskiing** is only allowed on stretches of water specially provided for the purpose and usually marked by buoys. It is also only allowed during the day and in good visibility. The tow boat and skier must keep clear of all other vessels. If another vessel is encountered the skier must keep within the wake of the tow boat.

Lights and Signals

Lights must be used between sunset and sunrise and in poor visibility. The following lights are recognised internationally (I):
- **All-round light** which can be seen from any direction.
- **Masthead light** which shines in an angle of 225°. Usually white.
- **Side lights** (green to starboard, red to port) which shine in an angle of 112.5°. Both side lights together form the same sized angle as the masthead light.
- **Stern light** which shines aft in an angle of 135°, completing a circle with the masthead light.

The following lights are recognised on European inland waters (EW):
- **Flashing light** which flashes at regular intervals (40–60 flashes per minute).
- **Alternating light** which is made up of two separate lights which circle round each other, shining alternately.

No other lights may be used which could be confused with the prescribed lights or which may detract from their visibility, or which may blind another boat.

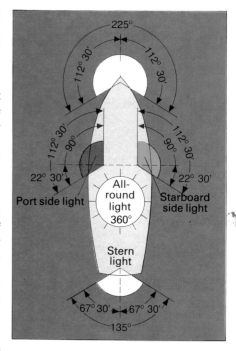

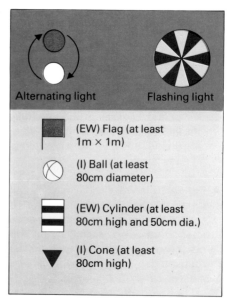

Alternating light   Flashing light

(EW) Flag (at least 1m × 1m)

(I) Ball (at least 80cm diameter)

(EW) Cylinder (at least 80cm high and 50cm dia.)

(I) Cone (at least 80cm high)

Rowing, sailing, motor boats

Rowing boats: white all-round light.

Sailing boats: under 15t under sail: white all-round light; when approaching other vessels a second white light.

 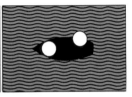

Sailing boats larger than 15t under sail: side lights (starboard — green, port — red) and stern light (white).

 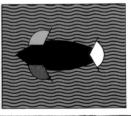

Sailing boats over 15t using both sails and motor: masthead light as well as side lights and stern light. During the day a black cone, apex downwards.

Motor boats under 15t (small vessels with motor): either masthead light (white) at same height as side lights and at least 1m in front of them, sidelights (green, red), stern light.

 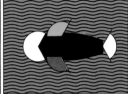

or
Masthead light (white) at least 1m higher than the side lights, side lights (green, red) on or near the bow, stern light (white).

 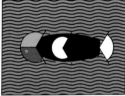

or
All-round light (white) instead of masthead and stern light, side lights (green, red) near the bow.

 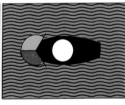

And on European inland waters:
Motor boats (small vessels with motor) over 10m long in daytime: white flag with horizontal red stripe.

Power-driven vessels, tugboats etc.

Power-driven vessels up to 110m long: masthead light (white), side lights (green, red) — at least 1m lower than masthead light, stern light (white).

 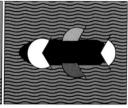

Power-driven vessels over 110m long: a second masthead light (white) on the stern and higher than the first.

 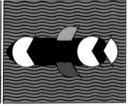

Chain or cable ferry: all round light (white), green round light 1m higher.

Ferry: as well as the white and green all-round lights, side lights (green, red) and stern light.

Formation of boats being pushed: three masthead lights (white, in the form of an equilateral triangle) on the bow of one vessel at the front; one masthead light (white) on the bow of each other vessel, whose entire width must be visible from the front; side lights (green, red) on the widest part and close to the pushing vessel; three sternlights (white).

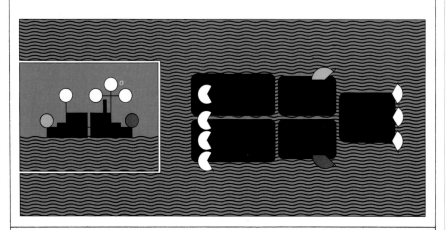

Towing formation and towing vessel: two masthead lights (white), one immediately above the other; side lights (green, red); stern light (yellow).

Towed vessel(s): all-round light (white), over 110m long a second all-round light behind. The last large vessel carries the stern light (white).

Daytime: towing boat: yellow cylinder with a black and white stripe at top and bottom.

Towed vessel(s): red flag with white square; last large vessel, yellow ball. (These special lights and flags are not used on small vessels!)

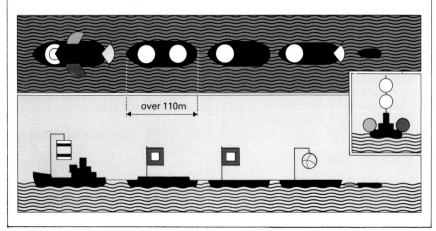

over 110m

Transporting dangerous substances

Vessels transporting inflammable substances: in addition to the prescribed light a blue all-round light. Daytime: blue cone (apex downwards).

Vessels transporting ammonia or similar substances: in addition to the prescribed lights two blue lights one above the other. Daytime: two blue cones one above the other (apexes downwards).

Vessels transporting explosive substances: in addition to the prescribed lights three blue lights one above the other. Daytime: three blue cones one above the other (apexes downwards).

Floating equipment — Non-moving

Floating equipment: vessels run aground or sunk: red over white round light on the navigable side (daytime: red/white flag), red round light on non-navigable side (daytime: red flag).

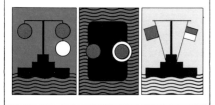

Vessels, floating equipment **to be protected from waves** (badly damaged vessels, vessels which cannot be moved): red over white round light (daytime: red/white flag) — as well as the other prescribed lights.

Motionless vessels: white all-round light on the navigable side. Vessels at anchor whose anchor could be dangerous: a second white all-round light. Daytime: a yellow float to mark position of anchor.

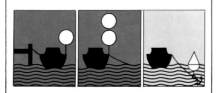

Police, different signals

Police vessels and fireboats: masthead light (white), side lights (green, red), sternlight (white); also (night and day) a blue flashing light.

Overtaker (does not apply to small vessels!): in addition to the other prescribed lights a white light on the bow visible from the front; in the daytime a light blue flag on the bow — till the vessel has finished overtaking.

Meeting another vessel head-on (does not apply to small vessels!): vessel going upstream must allow vessel going downstream to pass on the starboard side and must show to starboard: white flashing light; in daytime light blue flag. Or also by day and night, light blue flag together with a white flashing light.

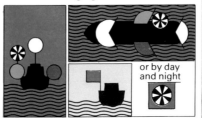

Vessels which cannot manoeuvre: in addition to the prescribed lights a waving red light. Daytime: red waving flag. In addition, or instead: sound signal of four short tones.

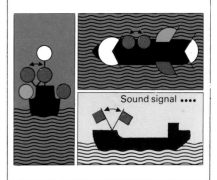

Vessel in distress: requiring assistance: by night a light, or in daytime a flag, is swung in a circle. In addition, or instead, a repeated long blast or a bell is rung.

Sound Signals

Sound signals are made up of combinations of short (●) or long (━) blasts. On inland waterways these signals are only given when necessary and large vessels have no duty to give a sound signal to a small vessel. Small vessels are generally not required to give sound signals. They could, however, if necessary give the following signals:

If a vessel carrying explosives, inflammable, poisonous or radioactive substances finds itself in a dangerous situation and is likely to endanger others it should give the 'stay away' signal which consists of alternate short and long blasts.

● ━ ● ━ for at least 15 minutes	*Stay away signal*

Other sound signals used by large vessels:

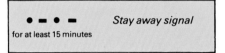

I wish to alter my course to port (when entering or leaving harbours or navigable lanes)

In **poor visibility** (e.g. fog) all vessels must use lights and regulate their speed according to the conditions. If sailing becomes dangerous a vessel must stop, leaving navigable lanes clear. **Fog signals** (not used by small vessels!) are as follows:

Signal	Meaning
━	Look out
●	I am altering my course to starboard
● ●	I am altering my course to port
● ● ●	I am going astern
● ● ● ●	I cannot manoeuvre
● ● ● ● ● ● ● ● (series of short blasts)	Danger of a collision

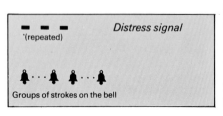

━ ━ ━ *Distress signal*
'(repeated)

Groups of strokes on the bell

Signal	Meaning
━ ●	I am going about to starboard
━ ● ●	I am going about to port
━ ━ ●	I wish to overtake on your starboard side
━ ━ ● ●	I wish to overtake on your port side
● ● ● ● ●	You may not overtake me
━ ━ ━	I wish to cross (when entering or leaving harbours or navigable lanes)
━ ━ ━ ●	I wish to alter my course to starboard (when entering or leaving harbours or navigable lanes)

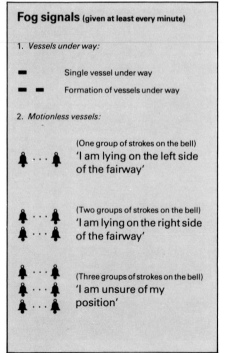

Fog signals (given at least every minute)

1. *Vessels under way:*

━ Single vessel under way

━ ━ Formation of vessels under way

2. *Motionless vessels:*

(One group of strokes on the bell)
'I am lying on the left side of the fairway'

(Two groups of strokes on the bell)
'I am lying on the right side of the fairway'

(Three groups of strokes on the bell)
'I am unsure of my position'

Water Traffic Signs (European inland waters)

A distinction is made between water traffic signs which restrict and those which recommend:

■ **Command signs**: square with red border with a black symbol in the centre.

■ **Prohibiting signs**: usually a square with a red border, black symbol in the centre and a diagonal red stripe.

■ **Instructional signs**: usually blue with a white symbol in the centre.

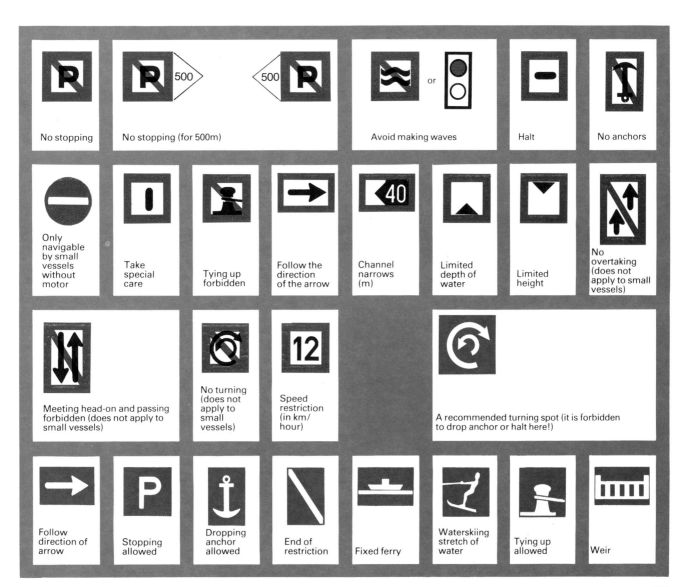

No stopping

No stopping (for 500m)

Avoid making waves

Halt

No anchors

Only navigable by small vessels without motor

Take special care

Tying up forbidden

Follow the direction of the arrow

Channel narrows (m)

Limited depth of water

Limited height

No overtaking (does not apply to small vessels)

Meeting head-on and passing forbidden (does not apply to small vessels)

No turning (does not apply to small vessels)

Speed restriction (in km/hour)

A recommended turning spot (it is forbidden to drop anchor or halt here!)

Follow direction of arrow

Stopping allowed

Dropping anchor allowed

End of restriction

Fixed ferry

Waterskiing stretch of water

Tying up allowed

Weir

Fairway Buoyage (European inland waters)

A fairway is the part of the waterway which is regularly used by traffic. Fairways are usually marked by buoys or beacons. On inland waterway lanes 'right' and 'left' are based on the direction the river flows downstream (from the source to the mouth).

Right side of fairway:
- Red flat buoys, or tall, thin post-shaped buoys.
- Coloured red/white at danger points or obstacles.
- Can have red cylinder as topmark.

Left side of fairway:
- Black cone-shaped buoys, thin post-shaped buoys.
- Coloured black/white at danger points or obstacles.
- Can have black cones as topmark (apexes upward).

Fairway divides:
- Red/black spherical buoys, post-shaped buoys. May have black/red sphere as topmark.
- Red/black beacons with red/black hourglass shape as topmark at danger points.

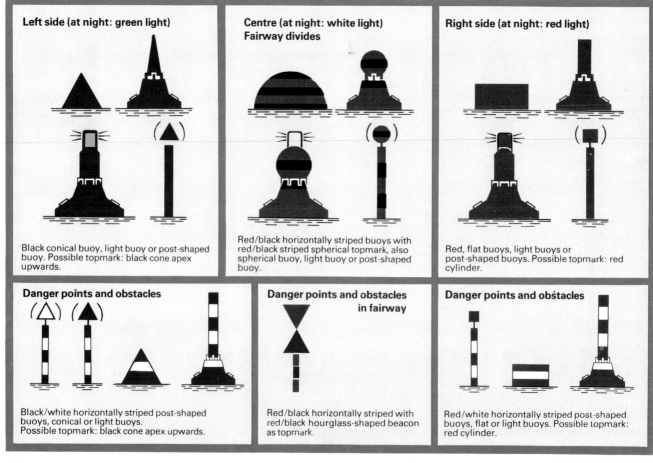

Left side (at night: green light)

Black conical buoy, light buoy or post-shaped buoy. Possible topmark: black cone apex upwards.

Centre (at night: white light)
Fairway divides

Red/black horizontally striped buoys with red/black striped spherical topmark, also spherical buoy, light buoy or post-shaped buoy.

Right side (at night: red light)

Red, flat buoys, light buoys or post-shaped buoys. Possible topmark: red cylinder.

Danger points and obstacles

Black/white horizontally striped post-shaped buoys, conical or light buoys. Possible topmark: black cone apex upwards.

Danger points and obstacles in fairway

Red/black horizontally striped with red/black hourglass-shaped beacon as topmark.

Danger points and obstacles

Red/white horizontally striped post-shaped buoys, flat or light buoys. Possible topmark: red cylinder.

Bridges — Weirs — Locks (European inland waterways)

The traffic flow under **bridges** is controlled by the use of lights, signs and flags. Red signals mean do not go through. Green signals mean you may go through.

Yellow or white/green diamond shapes show where you should go through; the red/white diamonds forbid a vessel to sail outside the lane marked by the signs.

Passage through a **weir opening** is only allowed when there is a green or yellow signal.

Entering and leaving a **lock** is controlled by lights. If there are several lock chambers, the vessel must use the chamber assigned to it by means of two special white lights situated next to each other both by day and by night (see diagram). If there are special locks available for small vessels, the large locks may only be used when it is impossible to use the smaller locks, because of the boat's measurements or the height of the water, for instance. If there is no small vessel lock available, then smaller vessels may only use the larger locks in groups or with larger vessels, except when a prescribed period has elapsed when smaller vessels may go through singly.

If you do not wish to use a lock, you may not moor close to it. Nor may you tie up beyond the halt sign on the bank. When sailing near to, or when entering or leaving, a lock:
1. Overtaking is absolutely forbidden.
2. Keep speed down.
3. Keep well away from other vessels.
4. Enter and leave after larger vessels.

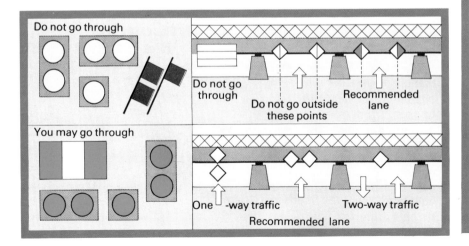

Yachting customs

Flags

Flags are four-cornered, while pennants are triangular in the ratio 3:2, or long and narrow, sometimes with a blunt end. Signals and messages can be sent using *flag signals* (alphabet flags and numeral pennants) according to the *International code of signals*. After the signal has been sent the flags must be taken in immediately.

Flags and pennants must be in perfect condition.

National flags: the national flag must be flown in shipping lanes, coastal waters, at sea, or in foreign waters. It does not have to be flown in British waters. On sloop-rigged boats it is flown at the stern; on multi-masted boats it is flown at the top of the after-most mast.

Visiting flag: after entering the territorial waters of a host country, yachts hoist the host country flag under the starboard spreader. It is regarded as impolite to hoist several visiting flags one on top of the other.

Club flag: this is flown at the top of the main mast day and night.

Flag Display: this is an international custom. The times all flags should be flown are: from 1 May to 30 September from 8.00 a.m. (9.00 a.m. during the other months) to sunset (or 9.00 p.m. at the latest).

Dressed overall: on festive occasions yachts in harbour or at anchor may fly international signal flags from the bow, over the masthead, to the stern.

Other yachting customs

These govern the manner in which a good sailor will conduct himself when carrying out his chosen sport. Many of these customs have come about because of expediency or safety requirements, and even sportsmanship and common courtesy have their part to play. This particular type of behaviour is very important — it makes sailing different from any other sport — and we take it very seriously.

A selection of yachting customs:

■ Sailing can be termed a team sport in which every participant must hold his own. This is even true for single-handed sailing (sailing on a one-man boat). If you have watched a Finn race and have seen how the 'opponents' help one another to unload their boats, you will understand what I mean. Comradeship is very important!
■ Noisiness, loud behaviour and blaring radio music are all unsportsmanlike.
■ Badly set sails, lines and fenders hanging overboard, a dirty boat and untidiness on board should never be seen.
■ Smoking? Why not! However, smoking is seen as unsporting behaviour when taking in, hoisting or folding the sail since ash could easily fall on the cloth. The result? A hole in your sail!
■ Bathing from the boat is not safe (except when the boat is at anchor).

■ Common courtesy and good manners should always be observed. For instance, you could show sailors from a strange boat where to berth and help them to do this.
■ Courtesy demands that when boarding a strange boat you should introduce yourselves to the owner or captain. On no account board a strange boat which has been left by the crew!
■ If you are alongside another boat and have to climb over it to reach land, you should take the utmost care to tread carefully.
■ Courtesy demands that you board a boat in the following order: youngest first, oldest (including women or important persons) last, and vice versa when disembarking.
■ Obviously a sailor should always help those in distress — as long as his action is not detrimental to his own safety.
■ It is unsportsmanlike behaviour when tying up to a jetty to spread your equipment all over the place so that it becomes a nuisance to others.
■ In strange harbours the master must immediately present himself to the harbourmaster to be assigned a berth.

8 Engines — Manoeuvring under Engine

How Different Engines Work

Petrol and Diesel Engines

Excluding the less common rotary and jet-propelled engines, engines are normally divided into two types: petrol or diesel engines. The most important differences in the way they function are as follows:

Petrol engines
- suck in a mixture of petrol and air;
- low compression;
- sparking plug combustion, the fuel being compressed in the carburettor.

Diesel engines
- suck in pure air;
- high compression;
- self-combustion by the injection of the diesel oil into the heated air (instead of carburettor — fuel injection system).

The advantages and disadvantages of a diesel engine as against a petrol engine are:

Advantages
Less risk of explosion because no electric sparks are involved and the fuel does not evaporate to produce combustible fumes. Reliable, more economical, higher life expectancy.

Disadvantages
More expensive, heavier and noisier. Of all the types of engine this is the most difficult to start by hand (two-stroke is the easiest).

Two- and four- stroke engines

The most important differences between these two types of petrol engines are:

Two-stroke
- Combustion at each turn, power stroke every second stroke.
- Burns petrol/oil mixture in the piston cylinder after low compression in the crank-case.
- Lubrication by oil added to petrol.
- No valves, no camshaft, lower performance to weight ratio.
- Higher consumption rate, less economical.

Four-stroke
- Combustion every second turn, power stroke every fourth stroke.
- Burns petrol after medium compression in cylinder.
- Lubrication by engine oil in crank case.
- More moving parts (e.g. two valves) per cylinder, somewhat higher performance to weight ratio.
- Lower consumption rate and more economical than two-stroke.

The **outboard engine** is commonly used as a secondary propulsion method on sailing boats and is usually two-stroke. This type of engine has a very good performance to weight ratio. It is simply hung onto the transom and secured by means of two clamps. Boats with very angled transoms can only use this type of engine with a special type of mounting bracket (see also *The Outboard Engine*).

Cooling System

Since very high temperatures are produced when combustion occurs in internal combustion engines, which could cause major damage to the engine itself, some sort of cooling system is essential. The cooling system extracts superfluous heat from the engine leaving only the amount of heat which will keep the engine at its most favourable operational temperature, which is about 80°C.

Most engines are water-cooled.

Basically there are two methods of cooling an engine: the direct and the indirect method.

In the **direct cooling system** water is pumped straight from the sea into the engine's cooling system and then out again. In the **indirect cooling system** the engine is initially cooled by an enclosed inner freshwater system, and then by a second seawater cooling system.

Advantages: the enclosed inner pipes do not get dirty so easily, there is no salt-water corrosion, anti-freeze additives can be used, and finally if something goes wrong, the temperature will not rise as fast as tends to happen with the direct cooling method.

Disadvantages: two pumps and more space are required.

The **hull** or **keel pipe cooling system** is a special type of indirect system where the heated water is pumped through a pipe running underneath the hull, or through a circuit running below the waterline along the underwater hull of the boat.

Note: Remember to open the sea cocks before starting the engine. Continually check that the cooling system is operating correctly by checking the outlet and temperature gauge.

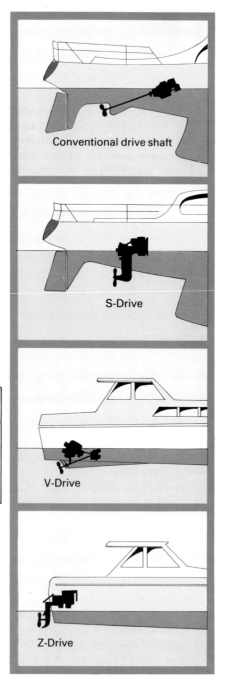

Conventional drive shaft

S-Drive

V-Drive

Z-Drive

Drive Shaft and Transmission

A reduction gearbox transfers the power from the engine to the propeller. This enables the propeller to be reversed and put into neutral gear. It also lowers the high engine revs to the lower propeller revolutions. The gear change can be operated by means of a **single gear lever** which serves as both throttle and gear, or by means of **two levers**, one to change gear and one for the throttle.

If you have the two-lever system you must be careful to reduce the revs by pulling the throttle back before changing gear.

The type of drive shaft used depends on the type of engine and how it is fitted in the boat.

Conventional drive shaft
Mainly found in sailing boats with inboard engines. The crankshaft, the reduction gearbox and the propeller shaft all form a straight line.

The shaft exits from the hull through a pipe called a **stern tube**. Water is prevented from entering the hull by means of a **stern tube gland**. This is usually attached to a grease cup which must be turned whenever the engine is used.

V-Drive
The drive shaft of the engine and the propeller shaft form an acute angle, the engine lying close to the propeller. This type is hardly ever used on a sail boat.

Z-Drive

This is used on motorboats only. The propeller shaft forms a Z-shape with the crankshaft. The engine is mounted inside the boat, and the driving leg lies outside behind the stern and can be moved around similarly to an outboard engine.

S-Drive

S-drive (Sail Drive) is a further development of the Z-drive specially for sail boats. It usually has a folding propeller.

Outboard engine

The drive shaft is vertical and works the horizontal propeller via bevel gears.

Propeller

Propellers are usually two-blade or three-blade. The two-blade propeller is most popular on sailing yachts because of its low water resistance. The *variable pitch* propeller and *folding propeller* have very good water resistance, though they are less efficient and more

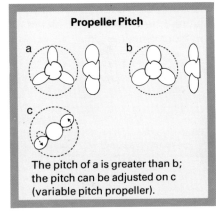

Propeller Pitch

a   b

c

The pitch of a is greater than b; the pitch can be adjusted on c (variable pitch propeller).

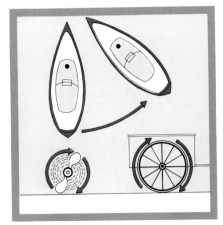

The propeller torque tends to pull the stern sideways (as if it were a wheel on the ground).

likely to go wrong because of the special mechanics involved. Both blades can be adjusted on a **variable pitch propeller** i.e. they can be adjusted to produce less resistance to water when sails are hoisted, or put into reverse position. The **folding propeller** is simply folded up when sails are hoisted. In order to get the best efficiency from a propeller the *pitch* must be appropriate to the diameter.

Propellers may be **clockwise rotating** (viewed from astern they turn clockwise in forward gear and anti-clockwise in reverse) or **anti-clockwise rotating** (vice versa).

The turning direction cannot be altered by fitting the propeller the other way round. Tied up with the direction of turn is the **propeller torque** which occurs on boats not steered by moving the propeller from side to side (outboard engines) but by means of the rudder blade. The power entering the propeller divides into two parts, one of which gives the required forward momentum, while the other tends to move the stern sideways. A clockwise rotating propeller will tend to pull the stern to the right (like a paddle wheel) and when in reverse to the left. The opposite occurs with propellers rotating anti-clockwise.

This propeller torque can easily be counteracted when steering forward at increasing speed by means of the rudder. However, when going astern the speed is lower and the paddle wheel action makes rudder control negligible. At first glance this would seem to cause all sorts of problems when manoeuvring; but the phenomenon can, in fact, be turned to advantage.

The Outboard Engine

To steer the boat an outboard engine is turned round its vertical axis. It can also be tilted up round its horizontal axis when not in use or when altering the angle in the water to improve the trim. As well as outboard engines with **short shafts** there are also engines with **long shafts** especially for boats with high transoms. However, long-shafted engines produce a higher water resistance and are more likely to touch bottom. A short shaft engine is the correct type to use if the *cavitation plate* (a device for preventing air being sucked into the propeller) is level with the bottom of the transom. If the blade is masked by the transom, you must use a long shaft engine.

■ When hand starting an outboard engine fitted with a gear change, make sure that it is out of gear or the boat could shoot away and cause an accident.
■ When you have finished sailing, before tilting the engine up you should close off the fuel while the engine is still running. By doing this you ensure the carburettor and float chamber will empty and you will stop petrol from spilling out and prevent sediment blocking nozzles. Quite apart from this you are polluting the water if the petrol/oil mixture is drained off.

Fuel Tank — Inspecting the Engine — Engine Failure

The Fuel Tank

Since you are dealing with inflammable fuel which becomes highly explosive when mixed with air, safety must be your primary consideration.
■ A remote fuel tank should be situated in an isolated part of the boat so if there is a leak the contents will not flood into the whole boat.
■ A valve on the tank ensures that if there is a leak in the piping the fuel will not spill into the bilge.
■ The fuel filler must have a close-fitting cap to prevent fuel or escaping fumes from getting below deck.
■ The tank should be well ventilated to stop fumes from escaping from the opening into the hull.

It is important that **diesel tanks** are not allowed to become completely empty or you will have to 'bleed' the air out of the fuel lines before the engine will work.

With portable **outboard engine tanks** the flexible tubing is attached to the engine and the carburettor is pumped full using a rubber-ball-type hand pump before starting the engine. Tanks sometimes have a screw in the top to release air — these should be opened before starting the engine to equalise pressure.

Refuelling

When refuelling you must be extremely

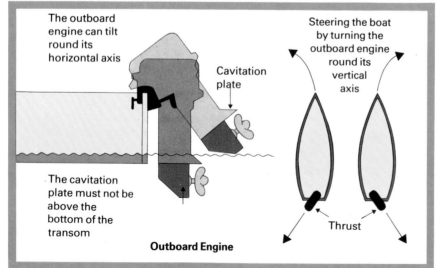

The outboard engine can tilt round its horizontal axis

Cavitation plate

The cavitation plate must not be above the bottom of the transom

Outboard Engine

Steering the boat by turning the outboard engine round its vertical axis

Thrust

careful:

- Close all hatches and windows to stop fumes.
- Put out all naked flames and do not smoke.
- Do not switch on any electricity.
- Avoid walking between boat and land.
- Ensure metal-to-metal contact between fuel nozzle and fuel inlet.

After refuelling:

- Open hatches and windows wide.
- Get plenty of fresh air inside the engine area by using blower.
- Wipe up any spilled fuel, rinse well with water.

You should never fill an outboard engine tank in the cockpit, but away from the boat altogether to prevent any fuel or fumes from entering the inside of the boat.

Here an outboard engine fuel tank is being refuelled outside the boat. If you did refuel on a boat such as this (open boat) there is no danger of any spilled fuel getting into the inside of the boat. However, a mixture of petrol/oil would be very slippery indeed!

Checking Engine

You should make the following checks before starting the engine, while the engine is running, and after switching off:

Before switching on	Ventilate engine area by means of blower, engage neutral, open fuel and cooling water valves, check level of fuel and oil.
Underway	Keep checking cooling water circulation and oil pressure, listen to the engine, and keep an eye on exhaust fumes. Do not make a cold engine race. Keep an eye on engine temperature.
After switching off	If applicable (not to diesel engines) close fuel stopcock and cooling water valves, switch off ignition and battery, put into neutral gear, check oil consumption, and, depending on drive shaft, check stern tube gland and grease cup.

Engine Failure

Unfortunately engines can go wrong for many different reasons. Always be very careful of the engine's working parts when trying to find the cause of a breakdown.

The following are typical examples of engine failure:

Symptoms	Possible Causes
Engine dies when put into gear	Blocked propeller, e.g. a rope or similar is caught up in it. Gear box jammed due to insufficient lubrication. Drive shaft jammed because it has been bent out of shape.
Revs increase, boat slows down	The power transmission between engine and propeller is cut off a) by damage to gear box (clutch does not engage), b) by broken drive shaft or keyway, c) by clutch slipping or defective shear-pin, meaning that the propeller is no longer driven by the drive shaft. Propeller lost.
Revs and speed decrease, diesel produces black smoke	A line, plastic bag or similar round propeller.
Outboard engine splutters and dies	Ventilation screw on tank not opened.

Docking and Getting Underway under Engine

Casting Off

Never cast off from a jetty under engine simply by applying hard rudder, otherwise your stern or bow is likely to collide with the jetty. The yacht must be a little way from the jetty to allow room for it to turn. In an off-shore wind or if there is a current coming from the front you simply push the bow away from the jetty after untying the forelines (wind or current will turn the bow even more!) and then untie the sternline, changing the rudder position from towards the jetty to the opposite side. If there is no off-shore wind or current to help you, make use of the propeller torque after pushing off with the boat hook. If the jetty is to starboard and the propeller moves in an anti-clockwise direction then engage forward gear, and if the jetty is to port engage reverse gear (see diagrams).

When casting off from a **buoy** slip foreline while in neutral, allowing the boat to drift astern till you are completely clear of the buoy, then untie the lines, put into gear and steer on required course.

Docking

The propeller torque must also be taken into account when approaching a mooring. Here we distinguish between

Left: Casting off with an anti-clockwise rotating propeller, jetty to starboard. Centre: Casting off with an anti-clockwise rotating propeller, jetty to port. Right: Casting off in an off-shore wind and with a current coming from the front.

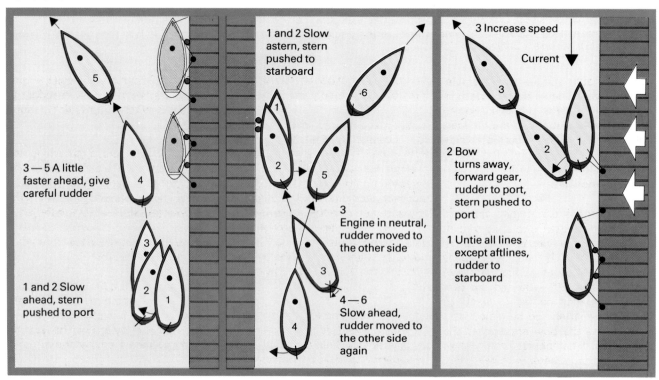

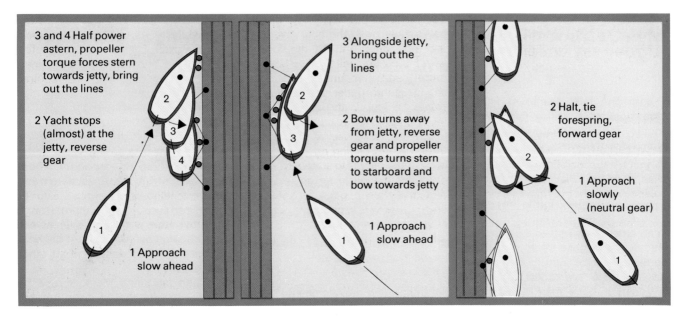

Left: Docking with anti-clockwise rotating propeller on the 'favourable' side. Centre: Docking with anti-clockwise rotating propeller on the 'unfavourable' side. Right: Docking with anti-clockwise rotating propeller into a gap on the 'unfavourable' side.

Within the figure:

Left panel:
3 and 4 Half power astern, propeller torque forces stern towards jetty, bring out the lines

2 Yacht stops (almost) at the jetty, reverse gear

1 Approach slow ahead

Centre panel:
3 Alongside jetty, bring out the lines

2 Bow turns away from jetty, reverse gear and propeller torque turns stern to starboard and bow towards jetty

1 Approach slow ahead

Right panel:
2 Halt, tie forespring, forward gear

1 Approach slowly (neutral gear)

---

the 'favourable' and the 'unfavourable' side for a yacht, depending on the turning direction of the propeller. For an anti-clockwise propeller the 'favourable' side would be the starboard side while the 'unfavourable' side would be port, and vice versa for clockwise rotating propellers.

To approach the 'favourable' starboard side for anti-clockwise rotating propellers, prepare the lines and fenders on · the starboard side and steer slowly towards the jetty at an acute angle of approximately 20° − 30°, having previously engaged neutral in plenty of time. The boat should be almost at a standstill as the bow approaches the jetty. Then, at half power, motor astern a little; the propeller torque will swing the stern towards the jetty. The fenders

should be put out on the bow first, then at the stern and finally amidships.

To approach the 'unfavourable' port side once again prepare lines and fenders on the port side and steer slowly towards the jetty at an acute angle, engaging neutral in good time. As you approach, steer first of all parallel to the jetty and then turn the bow away from it. Afterwards engage reverse gear and at half power motor astern a little with rudder to starboard; the stern will turn away and the bow will turn towards the jetty.

If you have to manoeuvre into a gap on the unfavourable side, you will have to use your lines to help you: approach in the usual way and slowly bring the bow to the jetty (fenders out!). Tie the fore-

spring first and then give quick engine bursts in forward gear with rudder to starboard until the stern is kicked round to the jetty.

If you find you are approaching the jetty too fast and the angle is too acute, there will be a danger that your stern (on the favourable side) or bow (on the unfavourable side) will bump the jetty.

If there is a current always make your approach into the current.

When tying up to a **buoy** take care not to motor over the buoy or it may get tangled up in your propeller. Always approach the buoy against the wind, or in strong currents, against the current.

Man Overboard Drill

If someone falls overboard from a motorboat or a sailing yacht under engine, the helmsman must do two things straight away:
- Put engine into neutral.
- Steer so the stern swings away from the person in the water to prevent him being injured by the propeller.

In an emergency immediately throw a lifebelt with smoke signal or a safety buoy with night light to the person. Never engage reverse gear to go back a few metres; quite apart from the danger to the person in the water from the propeller, steering a yacht astern is too inaccurate. You must turn in a circle, making use of the propeller torque by turning in the opposite direction to the way the propeller rotates. When approaching the man or practice dummy remember:

- The boat must come to a standstill to windward in a position where it is possible for the man or the dummy to be pulled on board amidships on the lee side. Flat motorboats tend to drift very quickly leewards and could seriously injure the person in the water. In this case it is necessary to keep the boat to leeward (there is then the problem of the boat drifting away so you cannot reach the person).
- The engine must be put into neutral and then switched off.

Simply putting the engine into neutral is not enough: it is easy for someone to knock the gear lever accidentally during the commotion of the rescue operation. And a running propeller can cause terrible injuries to a person coming into contact with it.

Towing and Rendering Assistance

Towing

A motorboat or a sailing yacht under engine wishing to tow another boat approaches from leeward or astern and passes to windward.

The tow rope is handed over as the motorboat is overtaking, or if the boat makes a short stop in front of the other boat's bow.
- When preparing the tow rope be very careful that it does not get caught up in the propeller.

The rope should be carefully and neatly laid on the deck so that there are no snags when it is paid out. When paying out, do not give too much slack but keep it uniformly taut, feeding it by hand over the cleat or bollard and letting that take the strain slowly. If the tow rope is belayed to a stern cleat, the pull will be one-sided and must be counteracted by giving counter-rudder. This can be remedied by tying two short lines to the tow rope (two slippery hitches) which are then belayed to port and starboard. You can also feed a line through the loop at the end of the tow rope and cleat to port and starboard. The use of this *yoke* divides the strain between several points and may also be used to take the strain off weak cleats.

Towing:
- In waves the length of the two ropes must be adjusted so both boats are

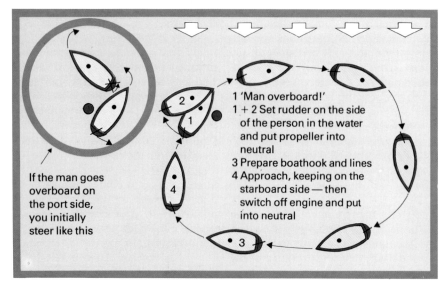

If the man goes overboard on the port side, you initially steer like this

1 'Man overboard!'
1 + 2 Set rudder on the side of the person in the water and put propeller into neutral
3 Prepare boathook and lines
4 Approach, keeping on the starboard side — then switch off engine and put into neutral

in the same wave phase.
- Keep away from the rope when tensioned: if it breaks it could swing back forcibly and might even cause a fatal injury.
- Do not travel faster than the critical speed of the boat being towed.

In narrow waters or in locks, a boat may be towed **alongside** if you tie both boats together by means of fore and sternlines and fore and aftsprings, remembering fenders for protection.

The stern of the towing boat should be astern of the boat being towed so that propeller and rudder can work freely.

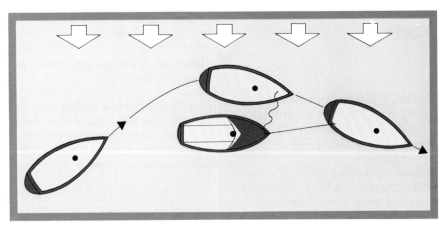

Rescuing a Dinghy

Approach a capsized dinghy under engine bow first to prevent any floating sheets, halyards etc. from getting tangled up in your propeller. By sailing close to the mast you may be able to lift it up and right the dinghy in this way. After putting the engine into neutral, you must first of all get anyone injured or exhausted on board, gather together floating articles, secure the righted boat with a line and then start towing if necessary. A dinghy full of water should be tipped up till the water drains out.

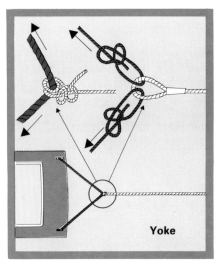

Yoke

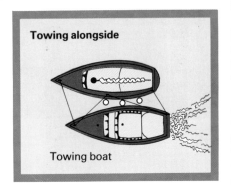

Towing alongside

Towing boat

Freeing a Grounded Boat

After being given the towrope go ahead slowly, gradually paying out the rope as you move. Shortly before the rope begins to take up the tension, put the engine into neutral, and after the rope has become taut, motor slow ahead again gradually increasing the revs. Remember:
- Divide strain on tow rope over several points.
- As long as the tow rope(s) is (are) under tension, keep well clear.

Once the boat is freed you should wait till it has been checked over to see if it is fit to sail.

If you wish to approach a keelboat which has grounded on a lee shore there is a special procedure to prevent you from doing the same!

At some distance away you should turn directly to windward upwind of the grounded boat and drop anchor. Then you should secure a line to a rescue buoy or life-jacket or similar and let it drift towards the grounded boat.

Locks

A lock is always entered and left under engine. If you do not have an engine it is sensible to get a tow or pull your boat in from the shore.

Preparing to enter a lock:
- Motorboats approach slow ahead, sailing boats take in sails and use engine.
- Put out fenders and take in other equipment which may be hanging over the side (e.g. anchor).
- Prepare lines and boathook.
- Close tie any tender being towed (or take on board).

Always enter a lock after any large vessels, keeping away till the last vessel has tied up. In the lock chamber the large vessels will produce a lot of waves. While the lock is working the lines must be slackened or tightened as appropriate, and in high locks they must be continually moved upwards and tied to the next stake on the lock wall.

- It is especially important to remember not to use a final twisted turn when belaying, or a clove hitch, so that you can untie your lines quickly.

Tying up alongside a large vessel has the advantage that you will not need to move your lines. However, you must be very careful not to get crushed between the ship and the lock wall.

In locks with sheet-piling walls, you must use a fender board: single fenders can easily get caught in the hollows in the wall and be torn off by the movement of the boat.

When leaving a lock always keep well away from large vessels as their propellers stir up the water so much you could be driven across the lock.

(See p.111 for lock lights system on European waterways.)

Turning in Restricted Space

This manoeuvre is essential in narrow harbours or waters. With an outboard engine or Z-drive engine you will have no problems since the whole propeller can be moved round making the boat very manoeuvrable. However, with an inboard engine you will have to use the propeller torque to help you. Without altering the rudder position, keep changing between forward and reverse gear. In order to succeed, however, you must know which way your propeller rotates! Always turn to port with an anti-clockwise rotating propeller and to starboard with a clockwise rotating propeller.

Turning in restricted space, with, for example, a clockwise rotating propeller. Slow ahead with starboard rudder and turn to position 2; then reverse; the propeller torque will pull the boat round to position 3; then forwards again, finally reverse and once more forwards.

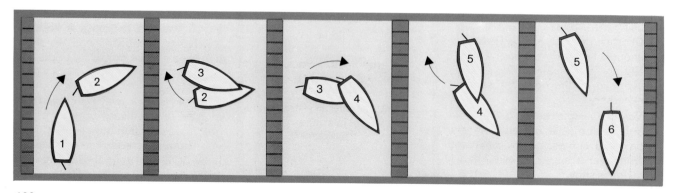

9 More Useful Information

Rules and Signals

Rules concerning Fairways

Fairways are navigable channels marked by buoys. They are meant for the through passage of vessels. The starboard side of a fairway is the side lying to starboard of the vessel entering.

The most important rules:
- A vessel on a fairway has **right of way** over other vessels entering, crossing or turning in a fairway, and vessels leaving their moorings or raising anchor.
- In a fairway vessels must **keep to the right**. Sailing boats may cross the fairway providing they do not hinder vessels which have right of way.
- **Outside a fairway** you must sail in such a way that it is clear you are not using the fairway.
- **Overtaking** is only allowed if there is enough room. Overtaking is basically on the left, although you may overtake on the right if absolutely necessary.
- **No overtaking** close to moving chain or cable ferries, in narrow channels, on blind curves, before locks and whenever a sign prohibiting overtaking is shown.

- If two powered vessels are going to **cross**, the rule is 'right before left', i.e. the vessel that has the other on her right-hand side must give way.

Traffic Separation Zones

These are a kind of motorway at sea where shipping sails on a one-way system on the right. Smaller yachts should try to avoid these lanes altogether, since ships travel along them very fast. However, you must be aware of the following rules:
- The greatest care should be taken when close to shipping lanes — you should keep as far away as possible.
- You must always follow the one-way system used by the general traffic.
- Keep well away (as far as possible) from the border areas.
- Entering and leaving is only permitted at the end of a shipping lane.
- Crossing should be avoided if at all possible.
- If you are forced to cross, it must be at right angles to the flow of traffic.
- A boat less than 20m long or a vessel under sail may not hinder a power vessel in a shipping lane.

Shipping Signals (European continent)

In the main these are identical with those used on inland waterways. However, there are one or two additional signals covering speed restrictions, unusual obstacles, closure of a lane and police halt signals.

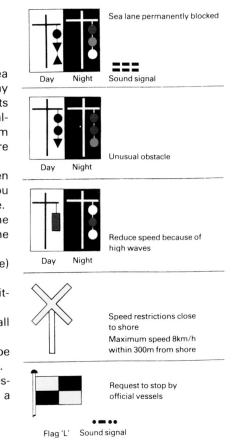

Day Night Sound signal — Sea lane permanently blocked

Day Night — Unusual obstacle

Day Night — Reduce speed because of high waves

Speed restrictions close to shore
Maximum speed 8km/h within 300m from shore

Request to stop by official vessels

Flag 'L' Sound signal

Lights and Shape Signals

As for inland waterways there are masthead lights, side lights, stern lights and all-round lights. The prescribed lights must be used between dusk and dawn and in poor visibility. Shape signals used during the day are black and can be ball-shaped, cone-shaped, diamond-shaped, cylindrical or hourglass-shaped.

With regard to lights used by sailing vessels, you must note the following: sailing vessels under 12m long must carry a white all-round light if it is impossible to fit the usual prescribed lights.

If a vessel is unable to carry a white all-round light it may not sail at night or in poor visibility. It must, however, carry a white light which can be shone in an emergency to prevent a collision.

Take great care in shipping lanes and do not hinder large vessels.

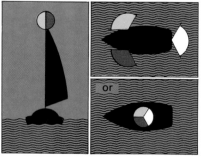

A **sailing boat underway** must carry side lights and a stern light.

On a sailing boat of **less than 12m in length** the sidelights and sternlight may be combined in one lantern which is carried at, or near, the top of the mast where it can best be seen.

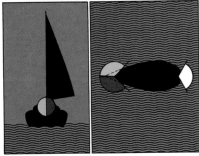

On a sailing boat under 20m in length the two sidelights may be combined in a **two-colour lantern** at the bow.

A sailing boat underway, **in addition** to the prescribed lights, must carry two all-round lights one above the other at, or near, the mast head, the top light red and the bottom light green. These lights may not be carried at the same time as a three-colour lantern.

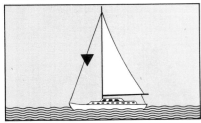

A vessel proceeding under sail and engine shall exhibit forward where it can best be seen a conical shape, apex downwards.

A power-driven vessel of **less than 50m in length** underway carries a masthead light forward, sidelights and a sternlight.

A power-driven vessel of **50m or longer** shall in addition, while underway, carry a second masthead light further aft and higher than the first.

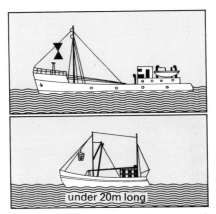

under 20m long

By day trawling vessels, and those vessels engaged in fishing other than trawling, shall carry a shape consisting of two cones with their apexes together in a vertical line one above the other. Instead of this shape vessels under 20m in length may carry a basket.

Lateral System

The lateral system is used to mark the sides and centre of fairways, and also any danger spots.

Starboard side (from the sea):
■ Green conical and light buoys — sometimes also with a green cone as topmark (apex upwards). In shallows, pole-shaped buoys (brush downwards). Also numbered (odd numbers) and sometimes having small letters as well.

Port side:
■ Red can-shaped light and pole-shaped buoys — sometimes also with a red cylinder as topmark. In shallows — post buoys (brush upwards). Numbers — even (sometimes also small letters).

Mid channel:
■ Vertical red/white striped spherical, light or pole-shaped buoys. Sometimes with a red ball as topmark. Also used at entrances to fairways or diversions.

Underwater dangers
■ These buoys mark individual danger spots and can be passed on all sides. They may be black light buoys, beacons, post-shaped buoys or poles with a wide horizontal red stripe. Topmark — two black balls.

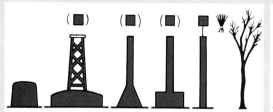

Port side of the fairway

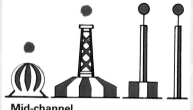

Mid-channel

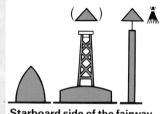

Starboard side of the fairway

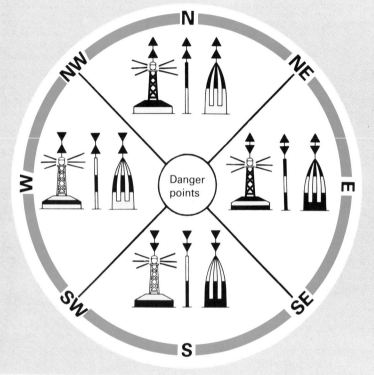

Danger points

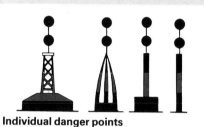

Individual danger points

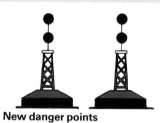

New danger points

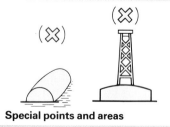

Special points and areas

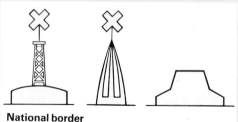

National border

Prohibited area (military or civil)

Cardinal System

General danger areas (shallows, wrecks) are marked by a system of directional buoys known as the **cardinal system**. These buoys show on which side to pass according to the points of the compass, i.e. the buoys are placed north, east, south and west of the danger spot. The markers are always yellow/black and have two black cones as topmarks.
- North: Black over yellow, cones with apexes upwards.
- East: Black with yellow stripe, cones with apexes away from each other.
- South: Yellow over black, cones with apexes downwards.
- West: Yellow with black stripe, cones with apexes towards each other.

Special Buoys

There are special buoys to mark dredging spots, military practice zones, bathing beaches, areas prohibited to civilians, etc. These differently shaped buoys are yellow and may also be post-shaped, sometimes with a red stripe or cross. Sometimes also a yellow diagonal cross as topmark.

New Danger Zones

New dangers which do not yet appear on charts or in nautical publications are marked by individual danger buoys or general danger buoys. In the case of an important new hazard, the buoys are doubled if possible.

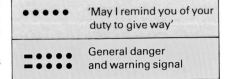

Signals

Sound Signals

●●●●●	'May I remind you of your duty to give way'
▬▬●●● ▬▬●●●	General danger and warning signal

The following signals in **poor visibility** (fog, heavy rain and snow) are not required to be given by boats under 12m long. Instead they should make a loud signal every two minutes.

🔔	One stroke of the bell
🔔	Bell rung for five seconds quickly
⊘	Gong rung for five seconds quickly

Fog signals — every two minutes

▬	Power-driven vessel underway
▬ ▬	Power-driven vessel with engines stopped
▬ ●●●	Towed vessel
▬ ●●	Vessel which cannot manoeuvre, sailing boat, fishing boat, towing boat

Fog signals — every minute

🔔	Vessel at anchor under 100m
🔔 ⊘	Vessel at anchor over 100m (gong at stern)
🔔🔔🔔🔔🔔🔔🔔	Vessel aground under 100m
🔔🔔🔔🔔🔔🔔🔔 ⊘	Vessel aground over 100m
🔔🔔🔔🔔🔔	Vessel lying across fairway or aground under 100m
🔔🔔🔔🔔🔔 ⊘	Vessel lying across fairway or aground over 100m
🔔🔔🔔🔔 🔔🔔🔔	Vessel lying at shipping lane obstacle or buoy — on the starboard side of the fairway
🔔🔔🔔 🔔🔔	Vessel lying at shipping lane obstacle etc. — on port side of the fairway
🔔🔔🔔🔔🔔 🔔🔔🔔🔔🔔	Vessel lying at shipping lane obstacle etc. — in mid-channel

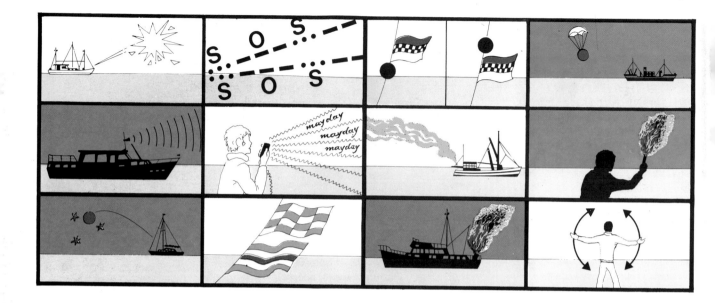

Distress Signals

Anyone who recognises a distress signal has a duty to respond to it. Distress signals may only be given in real emergencies. The following are internationally recognised:

A gun or other explosive signal. A continuous sounding fog horn. Rockets or shells, throwing red stars at short intervals. Morse code signal SOS (●●●━━━●●●). The word 'Mayday' repeated over the radio together with name of boat and position. The International Code Signal of distress indicated by the letter NC. A signal made by a square flag with a ball or similar object above or below it. A rocket parachute flare or red hand flare. An orange smoke signal. Slowly and repeatedly raising and lowering the arms outstretched to the side.

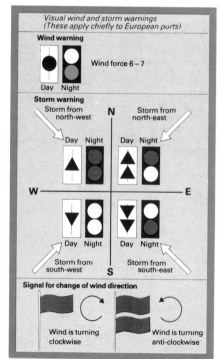

Visual wind and storm warnings
(These apply chiefly to European ports)

Wind warning
Wind force 6 – 7
Day   Night

Storm warning
N
Storm from north-west
Storm from north-east
W — E
Day Night   Day Night
Storm from south-west
Storm from south-east
S

Signal for change of wind direction
Wind is turning clockwise
Wind is turning anti-clockwise

Wind and Storm Warning

Meteorological stations will give wind (force 6—7) and storm (force 8 and upwards) warnings. These warnings are given not only over the radio but also as internationally recognised visual signals. You can find the position of your nearest storm warning station on a chart, in an appendix to a list of lights and in nautical almanacs such as 'Reeds' or 'Silk Cut'.

These signals are being replaced more and more by radio warnings.

Appendix

Transporting the Boat

Dinghies and small keelboats are usually transported on trailers. Small, light dinghies may be carried on a roof rack. The boat must, of course, be properly protected and securely fastened, and must comply with European regulations governing boat transportation, the most important of which are given below:

Roof Rack
- **Maximum width:** up to 2.5m. If the boat extends sideways more than 40cm beyond the outside edge of the headlights it must have lights fitted at night (white at front, red at rear).
- **Total height:** maximum 4m.
- **At the front:** neither boat nor mast may project over the car.
- **At the rear:** the load may project 1.5m beyond the rear lights.
- **Markings:** if the boat projects at the rear during the day it must carry a red flag measuring at least 30 x 30cm or a red cylinder 35cm in diameter and 30cm high, no higher than 1.5m above the road.
- **Weight:** the permitted roof rack weight on most cars is about 60kg. If in doubt check with the car manufacturer.
- **Speed limit:** there is no special speed limit for cars with roof racks. However, since the boat will produce a pronounced lift, it is very risky to drive too fast.

Trailers
- **Licences:** no special licences or taxes are necessary so long as the trailer is used for boat transport only.
- **Equipment:** heavy trailers must be fitted with brakes and tail-lights, indicators, reflectors, number plates and manufacturer's plate.
- **Length:** no greater than 12m from the rear of the car, maximum total length of car and trailer to be no greater than 20m.
- **Width, height, projection at front and rear:** the same regulations apply as for a roof rack.
- **Weight:** a trailer with no brakes may not exceed a total weight of 750kg.
- **Speed limit:** on the continent this is usually 80km/hour. In the British Isles it is 50mph with '50' stickers displayed. Heavy load 40 mph.

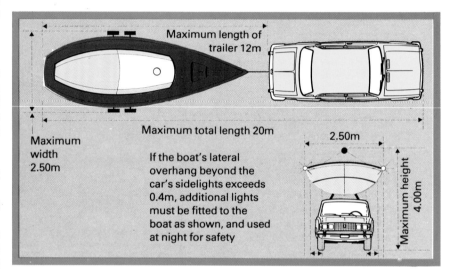

Maximum length of trailer 12m

Maximum width 2.50m

Maximum total length 20m

If the boat's lateral overhang beyond the car's sidelights exceeds 0.4m, additional lights must be fitted to the boat as shown, and used at night for safety

2.50m

Maximum height 4.00m

Conservation

Protect the environment as much as possible with these simple rules:

1. Avoid sailing into reeds, rushes or any other part of the bank where there is thick growth.
   Avoid shingle and mud banks (bird resting places).
   Avoid shallow waters (spawning grounds), especially where plants are growing.

2. Keep a good distance away from reeds, rushes and other parts of the bank where there is thick growth — on large rivers this distance should be 30–50m. Keep well away from groups of birds in the water — if possible more than 100m.

3. In nature reserve areas adhere strictly to the rules and regulations. It is quite common for water sports to be prohibited all the year round in some nature reserves or allowed at specific times only under certain strict conditions. Wild water canoeists may not under any circumstances change the river bed by, for instance, moving rocks.

4. Take great care in 'Waters of International Importance'. These areas contain rare plants and animals and must be especially protected.

5. Use the landing places provided or choose a spot where you are sure you will do no damage.

6. When on land, too, stay away from reeds or any thick vegetation on the bank to avoid disturbing the birds, fishes, small animals and plants living there.

7. In shallows avoid banks used by seals: they may bite back! Keep at least 300–500m away from seal banks and birds' nesting places. You should in any case remain close to the marked fairway.
   Keep your speed right down.

8. Observe and photograph animals only from a distance.

9. Keep the water clean. Waste should not be emptied in the water (e.g. the contents of a chemical toilet). This waste and any used oil must be emptied at the special collecting points in harbour.
   Turn your engine off when not using it to prevent unnecessary contamination of the environment by exhaust fumes.

10. Always remember these rules. Make sure you are aware of any special rules relating to the area where you are going to sail and make it your business to let young people and less informed sailors know, both by telling them and through your own example.
    By these means, we can all protect the environment.

'Teach Yourself' Programme

These are a series of exercises designed to help you learn how to sail better and more easily. They should also increase your general knowledge of a boat's equipment, and how it works. So they should make the path to perfect sailing that much more enjoyable! The author has devised this programme for students to practise on their own, after testing it thoroughly on his own students.

These exercises were developed by spending time on board with students, and are intended as an ideal method for the student to practise on his own. As a result, uninteresting and sometimes unsuccessful exercises suddenly became more interesting and exciting, so that the student unconsciously assimilated a large amount of knowledge in a much shorter time. The students who carefully followed the programme soon streaked ahead of those who decided not to bother.

Since the programme has proved so successful, we now offer it to all interested sailing students. One tip, though: if you want to take the relevant section of the book on board for reference, it would be better to copy it out and put it in a plastic folder to protect it from the spray.

Getting used to the Boat, Learning how to Steer

The following exercises are for beginners and very inexperienced sailors.

They should be carried out on dinghies only, with paddles and no sails (1–2 people paddling, 1 person steering). Ideal for calm waters!

1. Paddle forwards, then turn round 360° to starboard and to port (paddle on the outside of the circle!).
2. Make a figure of eight.
3. Paddle astern and steer in S curves.
4. Paddle astern then turn round 360° (starboard and port).
5. Paddle astern and execute a figure of eight.
6. Turn motionless boat: tiller amidships, then push away hard producing turning momentum.
7. If there are some buoys or posts at hand, slalom forwards, being careful not to touch the buoys or posts.
8. As 7 but paddling astern.
9. Steer to a jetty without touching the posts.
10. Describe S curves parallel to the jetty: steer in as close as you can then carefully turn away — without touching the jetty.
11. As 10 but paddling astern.
12. Steer a 90° course towards the jetty then quickly turn and go alongside.
13. As 12 but carry out the whole manoeuvre with raised centreboard (you will make leeway when you describe a curve, which will help the docking manoeuvre).

Close-hauled

1. From a close-hauled course free sheets and drift, then slowly tighten the sheets till the sail stops fluttering.
2. From a close-hauled course, luff up a little with cleated sheets till the jib's luff starts to lift and also the luff of the mainsail; then bear away a little again.
3. Sail with mainsheet cleated; counteract the tendency of the boat to heel (in a gust) by luffing up only.
4. Sail with mainsheet cleated: counteract the tendency of the boat to heel by shifting your weight only (sitting out).
5. Keep course and sitting position: counteract the tendency of the boat to heel by easing mainsheet only.
6. In a light breeze with gentle gusts: sail with cleated mainsheet and eyes shut, trying to feel the boat heeling and counteracting it by luffing up.

Downwind — Gybing

1. Move the sails to the 'goosewing' position, sail before the wind and steer to keep the foresail opposite the mainsail in a good position.
2. Sail before the wind on a curved path: steer so that the eased mainsail blows out over to the other side, then luff up again, etc.
3. As for 2 but steer standing up (tiller between legs).

4. Pull the sail over to the other side (gybing) on a run, both standing and kneeling.
5. Gybe on the run several times with tiller between the legs, tightening and easing the mainsheet using both hands.
6. Gybing round a buoy.
7. Sailing in a circle (besides turning, gybing is also required).

Head to Wind

1. Go head to wind from a close-hauled course; before the boat completely stops, bear away on a close-hauled course again.
2. Go head to wind from a close-hauled course and drift, back jib, and then sail on a close-hauled course again.
3. Go head to wind from all the courses.
4. Go head to wind to a buoy from all courses.
5. Go head to wind to a buoy from a beam reach, braking by holding the mainsail aback.
6. Go head to wind to a buoy from a beam reach, giving gentle rudder and noticing how far the boat drifts.
7. As for 6 but giving firmer rudder.
8. From a close-hauled course ease sheets and drift (almost head to wind).
9. Go almost head to wind to a buoy (from a close-hauled course and then from a beam reach).
10. Go almost head to wind to a buoy, purposely stopping

short, then pick up speed again by short tugs on the mainsail, sheeting in, easing, etc. ('gybe all standing').
11. Approach a jetty head to wind (if you are approaching too fast turn away!).
12. Approach a jetty head to wind, braking by backing the mainsail so that the boat comes to a standstill without having to be pushed off from the jetty.
13. Approach a jetty almost head to wind, stop short and move forwards again by short tugs on the mainsail.

Note: When leaving a jetty do not forget: back jib, correct rudder position when going astern, turn bow away from obstacle.

Heaving to

1. From a close-hauled or beam reach course, free sheets and drift, then back jib and give windward rudder.
2. From any course shoot into the wind, wait till the boat comes to a standstill and then turn out of the wind.
   Back jib and luff up.
3. As for 2 but stop more quickly by backing the mainsail.
4. As for 2 and 3 but determine beforehand on which side the boat is going to heave to.
5. Heave to from going about (foresail remains sheeted, main sheet eased, bear away further than normal when going about, then tiller to leeward).
6. Only possible in light breezes:

heave to after going about, but purposely turn through the wind and heave to on the other tack.
7. As for 6 but stop yourself going through the wind again by giving fast, firm counter-rudder (tiller quickly amidships, then slowly to lee).
8. While heaving to, sheet in the mainsail to different degrees of tension, noticing the boat's reactions.

Sailing Astern

Most important when casting off!

1. Sail astern without sails, using paddles (see also *Getting used to the Boat . . .*).
2. Tie up to a buoy, then untie foreline and sail astern holding mainsail aback.
3. Approach a jetty head to wind, then push away astern, and let yourself drift astern, or pick up speed by backing the mainsail.
4. Go head to wind, drift on, then back mainsail and sail astern. If you are travelling too fast then ease mainsheet again.
5. Go head to wind, brake quickly by backing the mainsail, then ease mainsail, back mainsail again and sail astern.
6. Sail a long stretch astern during which time you should practise taking in and hoisting the mainsail.
7. Sail astern, brake fast, give counter-rudder, foresail back on the correct side, sheet in mainsail quickly.

8. Sail astern towards an obstacle, turning away just before you reach it (as for 7).

Man Overboard Drill — Tacking Round and Going Head to Wind

It is essential for this exercise that you feel confident at going about, tacking round, going head to wind and, with regard to exercises 9–11, heaving to.

1. As for man overboard drill with gybe.
2. As for man overboard drill with gybe.
3. As for man overboard drill with gybe.
4. On a close-hauled course, throw a dummy overboard and (after a few seconds) bear away to a beam reach or broad reach, luff up and go about, bear away again and go head to wind.
5. As for 4 but go almost head to wind **after** the direct head to wind point. Dummy to lee (in two-man boats about the position of the shrouds).
6. As for 5 but go almost head to wind **before** the direct head to wind point.
7. Broad reach course, throw dummy overboard, luff up and go about, bear away again and go head to wind as for 6.
8. As for 7 but from a run.
9. As for 6–8 but heave to when boat is close to dummy.
10. As for 6–8 but keep a safe distance of about 2–3m from the dummy to windward. Heave to and drift in.

11. Practise the manoeuvre by yourself (no help from crew), because this is what it will be like if a man really does fall overboard!

Man Overboard Drill — Gybing and Going Almost Head to Wind

It is essential for this exercise that you are confident of gybing, going head to wind and, for exercises 7–9, heaving to!

1. Steer towards an anchored buoy on a close-hauled course, ease the sheets in good time and let yourself drift in. Take note of how long the head to wind stretch is (buoy to lee).
2. As for 1 but stop short deliberately and manoeuvre the boat towards the buoy by short tugs on the mainsheet (as for 'gybe all standing').
3. On a reaching course go head to wind towards an anchored buoy a) initially going directly head to wind then b) going indirectly head to wind about 3–4 boat lengths beyond the direct head to wind point and then c) going indirectly head to wind about 3–4 boat lengths before the direct head to wind point.
4. Close-hauled course, throw dummy overboard, sail three boat lengths further on, bear away, gybe, luff up and go directly head to wind.
5. As for 4 but go indirectly head to wind **beyond** the head to wind point. Buoy to lee (on two-man boats about position of helms-

man).
6. As for 5 but go indirectly head to wind **before** the head to wind point.
7. As for 6 but also heave to.
8. As for 7 but keep a safe distance of about 2–3m from the dummy to windward. Heave to and drift in.
9. Perform the manoeuvre by yourself (no help from crew).

Note: Instead of the dummy being always to leeward while you are approaching head to wind, try practising it several times with the dummy to windward, making up your own mind as to the advantages and disadvantages of both methods.

Glossary

Abeam At the side; at right angles to the boat (athwart).

Amidships Centre of the boat.

Apparent wind The wind felt on a boat while underway. Combination of the true wind and the wind of the boat's own speed.

Astern Backwards, behind.

Babystay Additional forestay.

Back E.g. Back the jib — hold it against the wind.

Backstay A wire cable extending from the top of the mast to the rear of the boat to help hold the mast upright.

Bail To scoop out water.

Ballast Weight (iron, lead) used for stability.

Batten pockets Small, narrow pockets sewn into the leech of a sail to take the battens.

Bear away Turn to leeward. Opposite: luff up.

Bend on Attach sails to a spar. Opposite: take off.

Bight Loop of rope.

Bilge The lowest area in the boat, in which water, oil and dirt collect.

Block A housing made of wood, plastic or metal with one or more pulleys through which a line is fed.

Bollard Post or a type of cleat, on board or on land, for tying up.

Boom A timber (spar) on which the lower edge of the sail is fastened, e.g. main boom.

Boom crutch A support on which the boom rests when the sail is lowered.

Boom preventer Line running from boom end forwards to prevent the boom swinging over when sailing before the wind in heavy seas.

Bosun's chair A simple seat which can be used to hoist crew up the mast to work in the rigging.

Bottle rigging screw Fitting to tension the shrouds.

Bow and stern post Posts at bow and stern of a boat.

Bowsprit Long spar projecting from bow to which light weather sails are attached.

Broad reach Course between a beam reach and a run.

Bulkhead Partition across or along the interior of a boat.

Buoy Anchored floating object to which boats can be tied up, or which marks certain spots.

Cable Thick rope, e.g. anchor or tow cable.

Capsize When a boat turns on its side in the water.

Capstan Revolving winch.

Carry lee helm Tendency of a boat to turn away from the wind — to bear away.

Carvel Construction method with smooth outer skin.

Cat Rig with no foresail and one mainsail.

Caulk Stop up cracks and seams in the planking of a boat.

Centre-boarder Dinghy; small, stable sail boat which can capsize, with a removable centre-board instead of a ballasted keel.

Chafe Rub, damage by rubbing.

Choppy (of sea) Irregular waves.

Cleat Fitting to belay ropes.

Clew The lower back corner of a sail.

Clinker-built Wooden construction method with planks overlapping like tiles on a roof.

Coaming Ridge around the cockpit.

Cockpit Sitting area for the crew in a boat.

Cockpit cover Protective cover for boat.

Companion way Steps leading into the cabin.

Covering board The outermost deck plank.

Current drift Deviation from course caused by current.

Cruiser Yacht with enclosed accommodation.

Cunningham eye/tackle Tensioning device for the mainsail luff.

Deck The working platform over the hull of a boat.

De-rig Remove the mast and the standing and running rigging, e.g. for winter storage. Not to be confused with taking in sail!

Dinghy Capsizable but unsinkable centre-board boat.

Dinghy cruiser Centre-board boat with cabin.

Ease Slacken a line. Opposite: sheet in, hoist, haul in.

Eye Ring, hole.

Eye bolt Bolt with an eye.

Fairway Special marked channel in coastal waters or mouths of rivers for ships with large draught.

Fender Protection, hung over the side of a boat, from e.g. neighbouring boats.

Fittings Bits and pieces used on board, e.g. bolts, cleats, clips etc.

Floor timbers The timbers where the ribs are fixed to the keel.

Fluke The arm of an anchor.

Foot The bottom edge of a sail.

Foresail Sail set in front of the mainsail.

Forestay Wire rope to support the mast from the front.

Form stability Stability of a boat determined by the shape of the hull.

Freeboard The height of the ship's side above water.

Freer Favourable wind shift — blowing more from aft. Opposite: header.

Freshening Wind increasing in strength.

Galley Ship's kitchen.

Gel coat Outer layer on boats constructed of synthetic materials.

Genoa Very large foresail overlapping the mast.

Go about Turn the bow through the wind. Opposite: gybe.

Gooseneck Special universal joint between mast and main boom.

Gun tackle Smallest true handy-billy with a working ratio of 2:1.

Gunwale Upper edge of boat's side.

Gust Sudden increase in wind speed.

Guy Windward sheet of a spinnaker.

Gybe To alter course by turning through the wind. Opposite: to go about.

Halyard Rope used for raising and lowering a sail.

Handy-billy Block and tackle system.

Hard As much as possible, e.g. sail hard on the wind. *Also* a slipway.

Hard chine Angular construction method, e.g. Pirate.

Haul Pull tight, e.g. sheet in. Opposite: ease.

Hauling point The place where pulling on a line will have the greatest effect, e.g. the jibsheet.

Hawse-pipe Fitting at the edge of the deck to take lines or anchor chains.

Head Upper corner of a sail.

Header Unfavourable wind shift — blowing more from in front. Opposite: freer.

Head to wind Turning a boat into the wind to slow it down.

Heel Describes the movement of a boat leaning over.

Helmsman The person steering with the tiller.

Hoist Pull up. Opposite: lower.

Jib Standard foresail on a sail boat; on boats with several foresails the jib is the aftermost.

Jib-boom Boom attached to forestay to which a self-tacking headsail is secured.

Jibsheet Line to adjust the jib.

Keel The lowest longitudinal timber of a ship.

Keelson A strengthening timber lying on the keel.

Knots A measurement of a ship's speed in nautical miles per hour.

Lash Bind together.

Lateral plane Side view of the boat's underwater hull.

Lee The side away from the wind. Opposite: windward.

Leech The back edge of a sail.

Lee shore Dangerous position for a boat in an on-shore wind.

Leeway The sideways drift of a sailing boat caused by wind.

Lift Flap, e.g. the sail is *lifting*.

Log Measure the boat's speed.

Long tack When tacking, the long leg by which you approach your goal but do not gain windward advantage.

Loose-footed sail Sail attached to boom at tack and clew only.

Luff The front edge of a sail.

Luff up Turn into the wind. Opposite: bear away.

Main boom Boom to which the foot of the mainsail is attached.

Mainsheet A line used to adjust the mainsail, which has at least two blocks.

Mizzen Mizzen mast or mizzen sail. The aftermost mast or sail on multi-masted boats (e.g. a ketch).

Nautical mile Measurement of length equivalent to 1852m.

Off-shore Wind blowing from the shore towards the sea. Opposite: on-shore.

On-shore Wind blowing from the sea onto the shore. Opposite: off-shore.

Overhang The part of the bow or stern overhanging the waterline.

Overlap During a race, when neither of two boats is clear ahead or clear astern, i.e. when one boat cuts across an imaginary line across the stern of the other.

Pennant Triangular flag.

Port Viewed from astern, the left side. Colour of port light — red. Opposite: starboard.

Port tack When the boom is over the starboard side.

Preventer backstay Adjustable stay to support the mast, which runs from the mast aft to port and starboard.

Pulpit Protective rails on bow.

Reef To decrease the sail area.

Reefing claw Open ring which goes round the boom onto which the mainsheet pulley system is shackled, enabling mainsail to be roller reefed.

Reeve Pass a sheet through a block.

Rib Transverse timber.

Rig Put up the mast and standing rigging. Not to be confused with hoisting sail! Opposite: de-rig.

Rope tail Lower half of a wire halyard enabling sail to be hauled up by hand.

Round turn Wrapping a line round 360**8**.

Roving Fibreglass used as strengthening material in the G.R.P. construction method.

Rubbing strake Batten along the boat's side to protect the outer skin.

Rudder Steering foil attached to the stern.

Run A course before the wind.

Seizing Thin line for whipping.

Shackle Metal loop with a screw or spring bolt to fasten different parts together.

Shackle to/on Secure something with a shackle.

Shallows A shallow place in the water.

Sheer Slope of deck towards bow and stern.

Sheet Line used to adjust the sail.

Sheet in Tension the sail by pulling on the sheet. Opposite: ease.

Shelf The uppermost stringer.

Short scope Pull in the anchor chain to the point where the anchor is just holding.

Short tack When tacking, the shorter leg by which windward advantage is gained without getting nearer the goal.

Shroud Wire rope to support the mast from the side.

Shroud plate Fitting on the hull for securing a shroud.

Single-handed boat Boat for one man.

Sound To determine the water depth.

Sounding lead Lead weight on a marked line to measure water depth.

Spar Any timber other than the mast.

Splice Join rope by interweaving strands.

Spreaders Short spars attached at right angles to the mast to support and spread the shrouds.

Spring Tying-up line used as well as fore and aftlines.

Standing rigging Metal cables to hold the mast upright, e.g. shrouds and stays.

Starboard Viewed from astern, the right side of the boat. Side light — green. Opposite: port.

Starboard tack When boom is over the port side.

Stays Cables to support the mast along the length of the boat (e.g. forestay, backstay).

Step Fitting or hollow in the keelson to take the mast foot.

Strand (ply) A laid rope is made from several strands (three- or four-ply).

Stringer Strengthening timbers along the length of the boat.

Swing Swing backwards and forwards, e.g. swing at anchor.

Tack To sail a zig-zag course against the wind. *Also* lower front corner (near the mast) of a three-cornered sail.

Take off (sail) Remove a sail from a spar, or reduce sail by reefing.

Tender Not stable.

Thimble Metal ring fitted in loop of spliced rope to prevent chafing.

Thwart Seat in a boat.

Tiller Bar fitted to the head of the rudder for steering.

Topping lift A line running from the boom end upwards to the mast to support the boom when reefing or when sails are stowed.

Track The groove in the mast and main boom to take the sail.

Transom Flat part of the aftermost part of a boat.

Trimaran Triple-hulled boat.

Truck The top of the mast.

True wind The actual wind felt when standing still.

Trysail Small, heavy, triangular storm mainsail.

Veer Favourable wind change with wind blowing more from astern.

Warp A mooring line. *Also* to haul in another direction by rope attached to a fixed point.

Whipping Binding on a rope to prevent fraying.

Winch Drum with handle for winding.

Wind of the boat's own speed Wind felt e.g. on a motorboat travelling at speed, exactly opposite to the direction of travel and with a speed matching exactly that of the boat.

Windward The side facing the wind. Opposite: lee.

Yacht General: sport boat. Particular meaning: keelboat as opposed to a dinghy.

Yaw Fall off course, e.g. because waves are running high.

Yawl Two-masted yacht with the smaller stern mast outside the designed water-line.

Yoke A rope divided at one end, dividing tension between two or more points.

Index